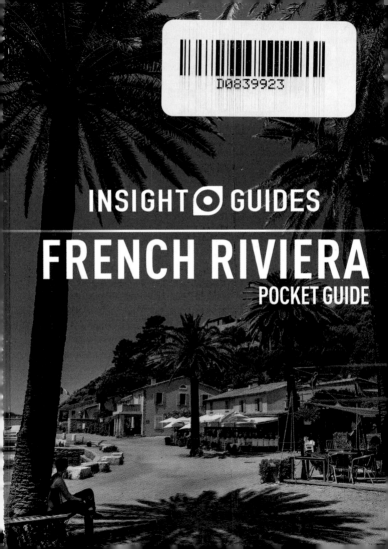

INSIGHT GUIDES

FRENCH RIVIERA

POCKET GUIDE

D0839923

◉ Walking Eye App

YOUR FREE EBOOK AVAILABLE THROUGH THE WALKING EYE APP

Your guide now includes a free eBook to your chosen destination, for the same great price as before. Simply download the Walking Eye App from the App Store or Google Play to access your free eBook.

HOW THE WALKING EYE APP WORKS

Through the Walking Eye App, you can purchase a range of eBooks and destination content. However, when you buy this book, you can download the corresponding eBook for free. Just see below in the grey panel where to find your free content and then scan the QR code at the bottom of this page.

Destinations: Download essential destination content featuring recommended sights and attractions, restaurants, hotels and an A–Z of practical information, all available for purchase.

Ships: Interested in ship reviews? Find independent reviews of river and ocean ships in this section, all available for purchase.

eBooks: You can download your free accompanying digital version of this guide here. You will also find a whole range of other eBooks, all available for purchase.

Free access to travel-related blog articles about different destinations, updated on a daily basis.

HOW THE EBOOKS WORK

The eBooks are provided in EPUB file format. Please note that you will need an eBook reader installed on your device to open the file. Many devices come with this as standard, but you may still need to install one manually from Google Play.

The eBook content is identical to the content in the printed guide.

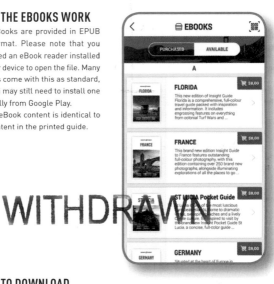

WITHDRAWN

HOW TO DOWNLOAD
THE WALKING EYE APP

1. Download the Walking Eye App from the App Store or Google Play.
2. Open the app and select the scanning function from the main menu.
3. Scan the QR code on this page – you will then be asked a security question to verify ownership of the book.
4. Once this has been verified, you will see your eBook in the purchased ebook section, where you will be able to download it.

Other destination apps and eBooks are available for purchase separately or are free with the purchase of the Insight Guide book.

TOP 10 ATTRACTIONS

MUSÉE JEAN COCTEAU COLLECTION SÉVERIN WUNDERMAN
New museum in Menton celebrating the work of the avant-garde writer, artist and film-maker. See page 39.

PLAGE DE PAMPELONNE
Miles of sand and great people-watching in St-Tropez. See page 74.

FONDATION MAEGHT
Beautiful presentation of world-class modern paintings and sculpture in St-Paul-de-Vence. See page 52.

CANNES
Serious glamour at the home of the world-famous film festival. See page 63.

DOMAINE DU RAYOL
Mediterranean gardens overhang the sea. See page 77.

MONACO
Gambling at the casino is far from the only attraction in the principality. See page 43.

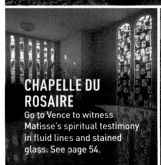

CHAPELLE DU ROSAIRE
Go to Vence to witness Matisse's spiritual testimony in fluid lines and stained glass. See page 54.

MASSIF D'ESTÉREL
An impressive landscape and a distinctive coastal route. See page 67.

VIEUX NICE
An atmospheric Italianate old town. See page 28.

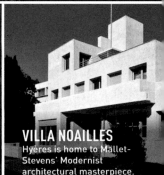

VILLA NOAILLES
Hyères is home to Mallet-Stevens' Modernist architectural masterpiece. See page 79.

A **PERFECT** TOUR OF

Day 1

City life
In Nice, stroll along the promenade des Anglais then wander through the narrow streets of the old town, checking out the market in cours Saleya. Buy a *pan bagnat* (see page 103) for lunch before heading up the hill to the château for a picnic with great views. Catch a bus to the Musée Matisse for an afternoon visit.

Day 3

Monaco
The best way to get from Nice to Monaco is by train (20 mins). Stroll along Port Hercule to reach place du Casino and the opera house. Enjoy a drink or lunch in the Café de Paris (see page 108), then flex your credit card in Le Métropole Shopping Center or catch a bus up to see the Palais Princier.

Day 4

Antibes and Grasse
After spending the night at Mas Djoliba (see page 134), amble through the old town of Antibes and visit the Musée Picasso. Marvel at the size of the superyachts in the port before catching a bus inland to Grasse to sniff around the Musée International de la Parfumerie. A locally grown rose or jasmine scent purchased from Fragonard, Molinard or Galimard makes an ideal souvenir.

Day 2

Paradise found
Take a bus or train from Nice to Villefranche-sur-Mer to see the Cocteau-painted Chapelle St-Pierre and the old town's covered medieval streets. Walk along the coastal path to Cap Ferrat then visit Villa Ephrussi's lovely gardens, before relaxing on Paloma Beach.

THE FRENCH RIVIERA

Day 5

A-list activities
Take the bus or train to Cannes, explore Forville market then stroll along the Croisette admiring the private beaches and luxury hotels. Indulge in a spot of shopping on rue d'Antibes then break for lunch at Aux Bons Enfants (see page 107). Catch a ferry over to one of the Iles de Lérins and drink in the views back over the coast.

Day 8

Hyères
Explore the old town of Hyères, including the triangular garden at Villa Noailles. Book a windsurfing lesson on the Giens peninsula or take the boat over to Ile de Porquerolles to ramble through the pines and eucalyptus trees, and picnic on the Caribbean-esque Plage d'Argent.

Day 6

Roman around
After taking the train to St-Raphaël, catch a bus or taxi to Fréjus and check into Hôtel L'Arena (see page 136). Visit the Roman arena and archaeology museum before hiring a bike to explore the Estérel hills.

Day 7

St-Tropez
Hop on a ferry from St-Raphaël or Ste-Maxime to St-Tropez, then enjoy a port-side coffee in Le Senequier (see page 73) before admiring the paintings in Musée de l'Annonciade. Spend the afternoon soaking up the sun on one of the public or private beaches on the Ramatuelle peninsula, before catching the train from St-Raphaël to Toulon and continuing on the bus to Hyères.

CONTENTS

INTRODUCTION

The French Riviera, Côte d'Azur, South of France – call it what you will – this, for more than a hundred years, has been one of the world's most idealised travel destinations. Written about, discussed at length, painted and photographed, it has as much glamour, prestige, charisma and wealth as any other coastline.

Real-estate values equal any in Europe, if not the world, and with good reason. Parts of the Riviera may have become over-developed, overcrowded and overexposed, but the area is not overrated. The setting is as beautiful as ever, and it still has an undeniable magic and inimitable appeal.

THE LIE OF THE LAND

Strictly speaking, the French Riviera is a very specific, limited area, extending from Cannes to Menton. In real terms, however, it includes everything from Toulon in the west to the Italian fron-tier in the east, including much of the mountainous hinterland. In fact, the French don't call this area the Riviera at all. They're more likely to say the 'Côte d'Azur', often taken to mean the whole of the Var and Alpes-Maritimes *départe-ments*, part of the larger PACA (Provence-Alpes-Côte d'Azur) administrative region, or the vaguer 'le Midi', designating the whole of the south.

However it is desig-nated, this corner of France

Artists' mecca

Given the bright colours and the quality of the light, it's no wonder that many artists have gravitated to the south. Monet, Matisse, Renoir, Bonnard, Signac, Chagall and Picasso are just a few who have celebrated the French Riviera in their work.

encompasses a truly entrancing panorama of ever-changing landscapes, with sun-baked beaches, elegant resorts, historic towns and picturesque ports. The traveller can also discover precipitous cliffs and craggy outcrops, secret bays and hidden inlets, wild, unexplored mountains and arid hillsides, vineyards, cypresses and silvery olive groves, medieval villages perched on hillsides, and

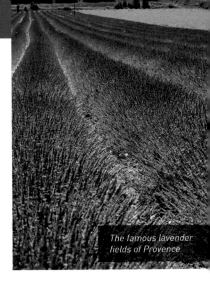

The famous lavender fields of Provence

ancient churches. Its past is charged with daring and adventure; today's traveller will find that even with the advent of long-haul flights and *autoroutes*, certain corners of the Riviera are still well away from the tourist circuit.

There is twice as much sunshine here as in Paris, even if out of season the climate is not always perfect. Winter has its share of cool or cold days, and there are often spectacular thunderstorms at the end of August. At any time of year the mischievous mistral wind can come raging down the Rhône Valley, freshening the vivid hues of Provence, but also exhausting inhabitants and discouraging beach-goers with its incessant, irritating roar.

Tourism is the area's largest industry, but it is not the only one. Others include perfume, ceramics, glass, boat-building and ready-to-wear clothing. In addition, the agricultural sector produces magnificent fruit and vegetables, olives, olive oil and wine for both domestic consumption and export. Since the mid-1960s and the creation of the business park at Sophia-Antipolis just outside Nice, the area has also become a major centre for high-tech industries.

THE PEOPLE

As for the local people, they have more in common with the easy-going, voluble Italians than with their cousins to the north. They speak with a rather drawn-out, lilting accent, and there are several local dialects, or patois, that are difficult for outsiders to understand. The general mood is carefree, and life tends to proceed at its own leisurely pace.

THE RIVIERA TODAY

Not all is sunny on the Riviera, however. Unemployment is higher than the national average, and differences between the rich and

⊘ LANGUE D'OC

An offshoot of Latin, Provençal began to take shape in the 4th century. By the 11th century it was widely spoken in the south, carried from Nice to Bordeaux by the troubadours. These roving ambassadors went from château to château, singing of idealised love. Both in style and theme, their poetry influenced the development of Western literature.

The language was known as occitan, because 'oc' rather than the northern 'oïl' (which became oui) was the word for 'yes'. After the 14th century, langue d'oc fragmented into regional dialects. In 1539, François I decreed that French should be used in all administrative matters.

Today you may hear a little Niçois, Monégasque or some other vestige of Provençal.

poor are sometimes at their most flagrant here. Mass tourism in the form of hotels, holiday apartments and villas has resulted in the sometimes disastrous *bétonisation* (concreting up) of much of the coast. Low wages, combined with rising property prices and competition from second-homers both from France and abroad, mean that finding a place to buy or rent can be hard for many locals.

Beach fronting the Promenade des Anglais, Nice

Every year, 34 million visitors come to Provence-Alpes-Côte d'Azur, but the Riviera is looking to widen its appeal, with the return of the winter season and short breaks, and the development of a more ecologically aware 'green' tourism in the less exploited inland areas.

Despite its historical allure, folklore festivals and picturesque villages, the Riviera remains a dynamic area: Nice and Cannes both have thriving congress and conference centres drawing year-round visitors; Sophia-Antipolis is an important hub for high-tech industry and research; Monaco is home to chemical, pharmaceutical and cosmetics plants as well as financial services; Grasse is a world focus for the perfume industry. Meanwhile, the high-speed TGV, which runs as far as Marseille, has brought the south of France closer to Paris and is being extended eastwards, while Nice airport is the second-busiest in France. Nice's tramway, which opened in 2007, is also being enhanced with the addition of two new lines and further development proposed.

A BRIEF HISTORY

The French Riviera was discovered very early on. Artefacts found at Beaulieu, Nice and the Grimaldi Grottoes in Monaco indicate that people lived here in Palaeolithic and Neolithic times. Around 1000BC, the Ligurians settled along the coast. They were displaced some four centuries later by Greek traders, the Phocaeans, who founded a colony at Marseille and trading outposts at La Ciotat, Hyères, Antibes and Nice.

Then, in 125BC, the Romans marched in, determined to create a passageway to their Iberian colony. They established *Provincia Narbonensis* (Provence) and founded several important cities, among them Aix in 123BC; Narbonne, the capital, further west in 118BC; Fréjus in 49BC, built by Caesar as a rival port to Marseille, and the garrison town of Vence.

The Greeks brought civilisation and agriculture – olive trees, fig trees and grapevines – to the area, while the Romans introduced their administrative systems, law and agricultural methods. Roman influence lasted for nearly six centuries, and during this period of relative peace, roads, towns and cities burgeoned all over the south of France.

Trophée des Alpes, La Turbie

THE DARK AGES

Christianity spread throughout the Mediterranean during the first centuries AD. In the 5th century the Church of Provence was formally organised along the lines of Roman administration.

However, as the Roman Empire declined, waves of Germanic tribes swept through the area during the 5th to 7th centuries, breaking down the established order and leaving chaos behind. The Franks prevailed, but Provence was more or less autonomous until the rule of Charles Martel. From 736 to 739, he took control of Avignon, Marseille and Arles, establishing his authority over the area.

Martel's grandson, Charlemagne, was the king of the Franks from 768 to 814. In 800, the warrior was crowned by the pope as head of a vast Holy Roman Empire that stretched from northern Spain to eastern Germany and Hungary. In 843, the empire was divided up among Charlemagne's grandsons: Provence, the area to the east of the Rhône, fell to Lothair I, and when his son, Charles, assumed control in 855, it became the Kingdom of Provence.

From the 8th century, the coast was often attacked by North African Muslims (also known as Moors or Saracens). In 884 they built a mountain base at La Garde-Freinet from which they raided neighbouring communities. Before they were driven out in the 10th century, these North Africans forced many local overlords and their followers to retreat into the hills – the

Trophée des Alpes

One of the most magnificent sights in the region is the Trophée des Alpes at La Turbie, which towers over the landscape, providing an enduring emblem of Roman power and self-confidence. On the base of the monument, a long inscription lists all the subjugated tribes of the region.

Provence penitents

There are Penitents' chapels in Nice, Cannes and Sospel. These were lay brotherhoods that appeared in the 14th century and proliferated across the Midi. They were denoted by the colours of their hoods, the most important being Pénitents Gris, Blancs and Noirs, and were devoted to sacred and charitable duties.

origin of the perched village strongholds (known as *villages perchés*) that dot the Midi today.

COUNTS OF PROVENCE

The situation improved under Guillaume, generally regarded as the founder of Provence, and his successors. With the North African Muslims out of the picture, the counts of Provence emerged as strong, independent rulers under the titular authority of the Holy Roman Empire. Trade and cultural activity revived, and the 12th and 13th centuries were the heyday of the troubadours, the period when Provençal became the most important literary language of western Europe.

In the 12th century, Provence passed to the counts of Toulouse and was then divided by the counts of Barcelona. One particularly able Catalonian ruler, Raimond Bérenger V, reorganised and unified the Comté of Provence into a ministate. The people of Provence received both commercial benefits and greater liberty from their ambitious new ruler, who also became king of Naples and Sicily. In 1246 links with France were reinforced when Raimond Bérenger's daughter, Béatrix, married Charles of Anjou (brother of Louis IX of France).

The house of Anjou gained control in the 14th century, while other powers claimed new territories. One such force was the French-backed Pope Clément V, who, shunning Rome, made Avignon his residence in 1309. The ensuing period was a golden age for the city, which became a cultural centre. It remained the religious capital until 1377, when Pope Gregory XI returned to Rome. After his death, however, the 'Great Schism' arose between Italian and French factions, when two and sometimes three popes (one in Avignon) held court. The schism was ended in 1417 by the Council of Constance, which elected Martin V as the one true Pope.

FRENCH RULE

After various changes of ruling powers, most of Provence (including Aix and Marseille) came back under the control of the dukes of Anjou. Under the rule of René I (known as 'Good King René'), last heir to the Anjou house, Provence's economy, arts and literature flourished, centred on his court at Aix. In 1480, René left his domain to his nephew, who in turn named Louis XI, king of France, his successor. Thus, Provence became part of France in 1481. Nice, however, was ruled separately. The city had formed an alliance with the dukes of Savoy in 1388, and remained Savoyard until 1860. The Var river formed the frontier between France to the west and the Comté of Nice and Kingdom of Monaco to the east.

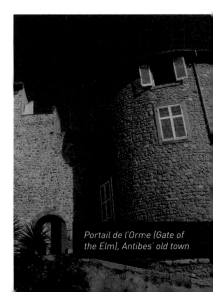

Portail de l'Orme (Gate of the Elm), Antibes' old town

The early 16th century saw strife between François I of France and Charles V, the Holy Roman emperor. François I fortified his frontier towns while the duke of Savoy built the citadel at Villefranche. Then Charles invaded Provence. In 1536, he took Aix and crowned himself king of Arles before being forced into a disastrous retreat.

In 1538, Pope Paul III managed to convince both sides to sign the Treaty of Nice, a precarious armistice at best. In 1543, helped by the Turks, François I bombarded Nice, which was allied to his rival through the house of Savoy. Nice repelled the invaders, returning to the realm of the house of Savoy.

WARS AND REVOLUTIONS

Meanwhile Europe had become the scene of religious conflicts caused by the rise of Protestantism. The confrontations, known as the Wars of Religion, were especially bloody in the south of France. In 1545, more than 20 'heretic' villages in the Luberon, north of Aix, were levelled by order of François I; in the years that followed there was much violence on both sides. The Riviera area remained mainly Catholic; in Vence the townspeople threw out their reformist bishop and the town was subsequently besieged by Huguenot troops in 1592. Finally, King Henri IV's conversion to Catholicism and the Edict of Nantes (1598), granting religious freedom to the Protestants, palliated the situation. (The Edict was revoked by Louis XIV in 1685.)

In the 17th century, Cardinal Richelieu, Louis XIII's adviser, made the consolidation of the French state his priority. Measures to increase centralisation and introduce new taxes gave rise to much agitation. Under Louis XIV, Marseille, Antibes and Toulon were converted into major ports and fortified by the king's brilliant military architect, Sébastien le Prestre, Marquis de Vauban.

During the 17th and 18th centuries, France took and lost Nice several times, but eventually gained some additional territory from the duke of Savoy. However, stagnation set in as power centred increasingly on Versailles and Paris. To add to the gloom, an outbreak of the plague swept through Provence in 1720, claiming 100,000 lives.

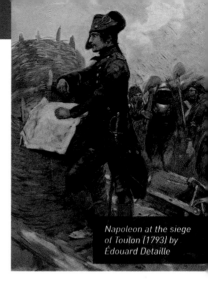

Napoleon at the siege of Toulon (1793) by Édouard Detaille

Like the rest of the French, the citizens of Provence had good reason to feel disgruntled by the end of the 18th century. Bad crops, poor administration and the distant court's constant drain on finance bred resentment. In July 1789, riots and massacres occurred throughout the south. The French Revolution was also a revolt against the Church and clergy: churches as well as châteaux were ransacked by the mob and confiscated by the state as *biens nationaux* (national property). In 1790, Provence was divided into three *départements* – the Var, Basses-Alpes and Bouches-du-Rhône – but the population was still starving, and fighting continued between royalists and republicans. In 1793, revolutionary troops took Nice, which remained annexed to France until 1814.

NAPOLEON IN THE SOUTH

Profiting from the disarray, the English easily took royalist Toulon in 1793. Napoleon Bonaparte, an obscure captain at the time, distinguished himself in the recapture of the city.

Promoted to general, he launched his Italian campaign from Nice (annexed by France from 1793 to 1814) in 1796.

Two years later, Toulon was the starting point for his sensational Egyptian campaign, and when he returned in 1799, he landed triumphantly at St-Raphaël. You can see a small pyramid there, erected to commemorate his victories.

However, his empire was unpopular in Provence – taxes and conscriptions were detested, and the blockade of Marseille proved disastrous for trade.

Napoleon passed through St-Raphaël again in 1814, but this time in disgrace, ignominiously escorted by Austrian and Russian troops on his way to exile on Elba. He escaped from his island prison a year later, landing at Golfe-Juan and returning to Paris via Cannes, Grasse, Digne and Gap – a road now known as the Route Napoléon.

The advent of the Orleanist monarchy in 1830, in the shape of Louis-Philippe, was greeted with relief. The revolution of 1848, however, took the south of France by storm, as peasants demanded the right to the land. The monarchy was deposed and replaced by the Second Republic.

By the end of 1848, Napoleon III had come to power. In 1860 the house of Savoy gave up Nice in return for the emperor's help in ousting the Austrians from the northern provinces of

Italy. In a plebiscite, the Niçois overwhelmingly proclaimed their desire to join France, although Monaco stayed apart as a hereditary monarchy. A year later, Monaco sold all rights to Menton and Roquebrune, which had also voted to join France.

THE 20TH CENTURY AND BEYOND

Southern France was scarcely involved in World War I, although its young men did have to go to war because of conscription. However, despite the construction of a line of Maginot forts along

⊙ FOLLIES OF FASHION

In the mid-1700s, the English discovered that the Riveria's winter climate was much to their taste, and by the end of the century it was a fashionable resort. Nice – and particularly Cimiez – was their favourite haunt, until Lord Brougham took a fancy to Cannes in 1834.

When French painter Paul Signac discovered St-Tropez at the end of the 19th century, other artists and writers joined him. By the beginning of the 20th century, the French Riviera was the playground of international 'high society' – princes, eastern potentates, heads of state, society hostesses and French courtesans all made merry every night of the hectic winter season with masked balls, gargantuan dinners, gambling in the casinos and fabulous parties.

Escaping prohibition back home, Americans arrived in the early 1920s, lured by the glamour of the coast and the low cost of an extravagant lifestyle. Based at Juan-les-Pins, they created the 'golden age' – they introduced jazz and crazy dances, indulged in wild parties and set the vogue for summering in southern France.

the Italian frontier, it could not escape World War II. In 1940, the Italians opened hostilities against France and succeeded in taking Menton. The Vichy Government of Maréchal Pétain was left to govern the rest of the area, until the Germans took over at the end of 1942, with the Italians occupying the French Riviera.

As the Allied forces approached from North Africa and Italy, the Germans put up blockhouses and barbed wire on the beaches; St-Tropez was dotted with mines. On 15 August 1944, the long-awaited landings began. The Americans swarmed over the beach to St-Raphaël and destroyed the blockhouses. The following day Général de Lattre de Tassigny landed with his Free French troops at St-Tropez. Provence was free.

The post-war years were marked by the depopulation of inland Provence and the population boom of Marseille and Nice, fuelled by the return of French settlers from Algeria in 1962. In 1936, the Front Populaire, France's first Socialist government, had introduced France's first paid holidays, heralding the change from travel as a luxury reserved for aristocracy and artists to tourism for the masses, a trend which accelerated in the 1960s and 70s. The tourism boom saw the construction of hotels, holiday apartments and campsites all along the coast, as the growth in private cars and air travel brought visitors from all over the world.

The late 20th and early 21st century saw the establishment of the Museum of Modern and Contemporary Art, a new theatre, and the Allianz Riviera stadium in Nice. Monaco's skyline soared with new skyscrapers and an additional district, Fontvieille, was formed. Still development continues using innovative and sustainable development techniques. Castle Hill in Nice has undergone a complete renovation, two extra tram lines are being added and a new exhibition centre is set to open by 2020.

HISTORICAL LANDMARKS

350BC Greeks establish a trading post at Nikaia (Nice).

125BC Romans establish *Provincia Narbonensis* (Provence).

49BC Julius Caesar creates a new port at Fréjus.

AD1309 Pope Clément V makes Avignon his residence.

1388 Comté of Nice becomes separate from France.

1481 Provence (but not Nice) becomes part of the French kingdom.

1538 Treaty of Nice between François I and Emperor Charles V.

1731 First English visitors 'winter' in Nice.

1789 Start of the French Revolution.

1814 Napoleon sails from St-Raphaël to exile in Elba.

1824 Nice's Promenade des Anglais built.

1860 Comtés of Nice, Menton and Roquebrune vote to rejoin France.

1873 First Nice Carnival during the two weeks prior to Lent.

1878 Casino opens in Monte Carlo.

1892 Artists' colony formed in St-Tropez.

1923 Creation of the summer season when the Hôtel du Cap at Juan-les-Pins stays open for the summer.

1942 Italy occupies French Riviera on behalf of Germany.

1944 Southern France liberated by Allies.

1946 First major Cannes Film Festival.

1956 Prince Rainier marries film star Grace Kelly.

1982 Princess Grace of Monaco dies in a car accident.

2001 The high-speed TGV rail network reaches Marseille.

2005 Prince Rainier of Monaco dies, succeeded by his son, Prince Albert.

2007 Tramway opens in Nice.

2011 Prince Albert of Monaco marries Charlene Wittstock.

2012 Socialist François Hollande is elected President of France.

2016 A truck is driven into a crowd on the Promenade des Anglais during the Bastille Day celebrations. 87 people are killed and over 200 injured. UEFA European Championship hosted in Nice.

2017 Emmanuel Macron is elected President of France.

2018 France wins the World Cup for the second time.

The beach at Cannes

WHERE TO GO

The French Riviera offers plenty for the visitor, from busy coastal resorts to tranquil hill villages, from Roman ruins to modern art icons. We start at Nice, unofficial capital of the French Riviera, then head eastwards up the coast to Menton on the Italian frontier and the principality of Monaco; then west of Nice to Antibes and Cannes, not forgetting to go inland to explore the artistic heritage of Vence and St-Paul. We continue west along the Var coast, via St-Tropez and the Maures mountains, to the gritty naval port of Toulon.

NICE

With a population of around 350,000, **Nice** ❶ is France's fifth largest city and home to its second-busiest airport, an opera house and excellent philharmonic orchestra, a university, several good museums, numerous shops, and hotels and restaurants to rival the world's best.

Phocaeans from Marseille settled here in the 4th century BC, and the name Nikaia (Nice) may have come from *nike*, the Greek word for victory. When the Romans marched in two centuries later, they headed for the healthier climes of the Cimiez hill, where they founded a city.

Nice broke away from the rest of Provence in 1388, when it was annexed by the house of Savoy (see page 17). When Provence joined France in 1481, Nice stayed apart, not joining France officially until 1860. In the 15th century, the hill now known as Le Château supported a fortified castle, and beneath it a city grew up (now known as Vieux Nice). The citizens of Nice were almost wiped out by the plague in 1631 – but the city survived. In 1796,

On the beach at Nice

when briefly under French rule again, the city was used by Napoleon Bonaparte as a base during his Italian campaign. Known as a winter resort since the late 1700s, Nice saw its touristic career take off in the next century, with the arrival of the English and their queen, Victoria, along with the Russian aristocracy.

It's easy to orientate yourself: Vieux Nice (Old Nice) clusters around Le Château, stretching as far as boulevard Jean Jaurès. Pedestrianised place Masséna marks the start of the modern city and its main thoroughfare, avenue Jean Médecin. To the north is Cimiez, and to the south, stretching westwards along the seafront, is the promenade des Anglais.

PROMENADE DES ANGLAIS

Any visit to Nice passes along this splendid palm-tree-lined boulevard, 5km (3 miles) in length. For most of the way, the promenade des Anglais – thus named because in the 1820s the widening of a coastal path was paid for by local English residents – runs beside the Mediterranean shoreline of the Baie des Anges. Halfway along is the **Negresco** (see page 139) – a stunning *belle époque* hotel with an imposing façade, colourful turrets and uniformed doormen. Next door, a permanent exhibition in the **Villa Masséna Ⓐ** (Wed–Mon 10am–6pm), a lavish villa built in1898 for the prince Victor Masséna, portrays the evolution of the town over the 19th century and the artists, writers and aristocrats who frequented it. A little further on, the **Palais de la Méditerranée** contains a modern casino and hotel behind a striking Art Deco façade.

At the eastern end of the promenade, where it joins the quai des Etats-Unis, is a park, the **Jardin Albert-1er**. Laid out in the late 19th century when the River Peillon was covered over, it features an 18th-century Triton fountain and a modern outdoor theatre. Behind the gardens, running parallel to the promenade, is a shopping area, mostly reserved for pedestrians. To the northeast of the park is **place Masséna**, a square of arcaded buildings in ruddy stucco, built in 1835.

Running behind the promenade des Anglais lies the **nouvelle ville** (new town), which grew up in the late 19th and early 20th centuries, laid out with garden squares, fanciful villas and *belle époque* and Art Deco apartment blocks and hotels. A couple of blocks west of the station, on avenue Nicolas II, the **Russian Orthodox Cathedral B** (Mon–Sat 9am–noon, 2–6pm) is Nice's most visited sight. Complete with five onion domes, precious icons and a gilded iconostasis (the screen that separates the space for the congregation from that reserved for the clergy), it is the largest Russian church outside Russia. Further west, on the Baumettes

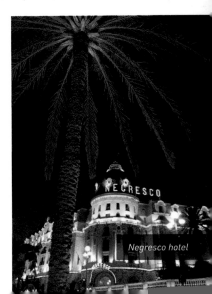

Negresco hotel

Nice's Russian Cathedral

hill, the often overlooked **Musée des Beaux-Arts de Nice** (www.musee-beaux-arts-nice.org; Tue–Sun 10am–6pm) occupies a grandiose mansion. The collection ranges from the late Middle Ages to the early 20th century, including scenes by Jan 'Velvet' Brueghel, an old man by Fragonard, plaster studies by Carpeaux, and whole rooms of Dufy, Van Dongen and pastellist Jules Cheret.

At the very westernmost end of the promenade, almost at Nice airport, is the exotic, flower-filled **Parc Phoenix** (daily Apr–Sept 9.30am–7.30pm, Oct–Mar 9.30am–6pm), home to one of the largest single-span glasshouses in Europe, at some 7,000 sq m (75,000 sq ft).

Set in a lake on the edge of the park, the **Musée des Arts Asiatiques** (www.arts-asiatiques.com; Wed–Mon July–Aug 10am–6pm, Sep–June 10am–5pm), in a spectacular circular building designed by Japanese architect Kenzo Tange, has a fine collection of Asian artefacts and a tearoom where Japanese and Chinese tea ceremonies are performed on alternate Sundays.

VIEUX NICE

You can enter the **vieille ville** (old town) from the seaside (quai des Etats-Unis) or place Masséna. From the latter, proceed past the **Opéra**, which has an elaborate 19th-century façade, and continue to **cours Saleya**. Lined with busy cafés and restaurants, this is where the flower market takes place, full of the colour and scent of roses, tulips, dahlias and geraniums (Tue–Sat 6am–5.30pm, Sun 6.30am–1.30pm), and the fruit-and-vegetable market (6am–1pm). Both markets are open daily, except Monday, when there is an antiques and bric-a-brac market from 7am to 6pm.

On the quayside, the little pastel houses where fishermen used to live (now mostly art galleries and restaurants) are known as *ponchettes*, a Provençal word meaning 'little rocks'. Opposite is the **Miséricorde** chapel (Tue 2.30–5pm, closed July–Aug). Built by the Black Penitents (a lay sect) in 1736, it contains an attractive altarpiece, *La Vierge de Miséricorde*, by Mirailhet.

Behind cours Saleya is an area reminiscent of Nice of yesteryear, with its appetising aromas, tiny shops spilling their wares onto the streets and excited voices talking Niçois, a form of Provençal. Nowadays, **rue Droite** looks like a cramped alleyway, but in the Middle Ages it was the city's main street. On the right is the **Eglise du Gésu** (Tue 3–7pm, Thu 3–5.30pm, Sat 9am–noon, 3–6pm), a lavish Baroque church modelled after Il Gesù in Rome. On the left, **Palais Lascaris D** (15 rue Droite; Wed–Mon 11am–6pm, end June–mid Oct 10am–6pm) is a 17th-century town house that belonged to the Lascaris family until the French Revolution. Although small for a palace, the building has frescoed ceilings and a handsome carved vaulted staircase painted with grotesques. The upper floors house a collection of historic musical instruments. On the ground floor is a beautifully preserved pharmacy from 1738, complete with apothecary jars. On lively place Rossetti you'll find **Cathédrale Ste-Réparate** (www.cathedrale-nice-fr; Tue–Fri 9am–noon, 2–6pm, Sat until 7.30pm, Sun 9am–1pm, 3–6pm), which has an impressive dome and handsome 18th-century belfry.

Further on you'll find place Saint François with its attractively proportioned, late-Baroque former town hall. Every morning except Monday, a frenetic fish market takes over the square, gleaming with red mullet, sea bass and squid.

Just outside the old town, on the promenade des Arts, are the Théâtre de Nice and the **Musée d'Art Moderne et d'Art Contemporain** ❻ (www.mamac-nice.org; Tue–Sun 10am–6pm), grouping modern and contemporary art with an emphasis on American pop art and the French *nouveaux réalistes*. A large donation by Nikki de Saint-Phalle includes her water-spouting mirror-mosaic *Loch Ness Monster* on the terrace outside. Nearby, Esplanade John-Fitzgerald-Kennedy is the site of the **Acropolis**, Nice's impressive exhibition and conference centre.

LE CHÂTEAU AND THE HARBOUR

Though you won't find anything left of Nice's stronghold of the Middle Ages – destroyed in 1706 – a visit to the 92m (300ft) summit of **Le Château** ❺ is pleasant nonetheless. Hardy walkers can

⊙ CARNIVAL CAVORTINGS

Nice's February Lenten carnival (www.nicecarnaval.com), or Mardi Gras, lasts for almost three weeks. Begun as a simple fête in the 13th century, the carnival was put on in splendid style in 1873; today, crowds jam the boulevards for the parades of floats in extravagant shapes and colours. The papier mâché used for the floats requires about a tonne of paper, plus 317kg (700lb) of flour. Masked parades and balls alternate with the battles of flowers and confetti. The climax is the Shrove Tuesday burning of King Carnival in effigy and a fireworks display, topped off by cannon volleys from the castle hill.

climb the steps in 15 minutes, but a free lift service also operates daily between 8am and 7pm (8am–6pm in winter) from the eastern end of quai des Etats-Unis. Alternatively, take the 'little train' (every 30 mins Oct–Mar 10am–5pm, Apr–May and Sept until 6pm, June–Aug until 7pm; closed on rainy days) that runs from opposite the Jardin Albert-1er through cours Saleya and the narrow streets of the old town. It is a highly

View of the port
from Le Château

enjoyable experience, especially if you leave the train at the top (it turns round and goes straight back down), have a drink in the café and come down by a later train. At the top there is a public park, with exotic pines and cacti, and a spectacular view of the colourful port on one side and the Baie des Anges on the other.

Filled with both pleasure and merchant boats, the lively **port** is lined with bars, cafés and restaurants specialising in the Niçois version of the delicious Mediterranean fish and seafood stew – bouillabaisse.

From the northeast corner of the harbour, you can take the boulevard Carnot to the **Musée d'Archéologie de Nice – Site de Terra Amata** (Wed–Sun mid-Oct–end June 11am–6pm, end June–mid Oct 10am–6pm), located at No. 25. Practically hidden under towering residential buildings, it contains a collection of prehistoric remains, found in a sand dune when the land was being cleared for construction. Around 400,000 years ago,

Inside Musée Matisse

men hunted on the shores that lie under these recent buildings.

CIMIEZ

Originally built by the Romans, the hilly residential suburb of **Cimiez** was much favoured by European aristocracy in the 19th century.

Within easy reach of Nice city centre, the route to Cimiez passes close to the **Musée National Marc Chagall** (www. en.nicetourisme.com; Wed–Mon May–Oct 10am–6pm, Nov–Apr until 5pm) on avenue Dr Ménard at the lower end of boulevard de Cimiez. The museum, originally designed to house Chagall's *Message Biblique*, is the biggest single collection of his work. At the top of the boulevard is the **Régina Palace**, the grandest of many *belle époque* hotels and villas and a favourite of Queen Victoria (Matisse spent his later life in an apartment here). Just beyond on avenue des Arènes, the **Musée Matisse** (www.musee-matisse-nice.org; Wed–Mon 10am–6pm) occupies a 17th-century villa and its modern extension. Works from all periods of Matisse's life are displayed, together with personal items from his studio.

Behind the villa, in a park planted with olive groves, you can walk around **Roman ruins**, part of the **Musée d'Archéologie de Nice – Site de Cemenelum** (Wed–Mon 10am–6pm). Across the road are the remains of a small amphitheatre (used for the Nice Jazz Festival each summer).

On the eastern side is a **Franciscan monastery** with a late Gothic church (Mon–Sat 10am–noon and 3–6pm). It contains three remarkable altarpieces painted on wood in the 15th century – the work of Louis Bréa. Both Matisse and Dufy are buried in the adjoining cemetery.

NICE EXCURSIONS

Nice is an excellent starting point for short trips along the French Riviera and into the wonderful hinterland.

If you enjoy spectacular scenery and mountain driving, take the day-long tour featuring the twin gorges of Daluis and Cians. Leaving Nice on the RN202, you will follow the River Var and pass through numerous medieval villages.

Entrevaux (72km/45 miles from Nice), a lovely fortified town, is well worth a visit. Then head for Guillaumes via the **Gorges de Daluis**, outstanding for their depth and red colouring. Stops including the ski resort of **Valberg** and the Alpine town of **Beuil** precede the **Gorges du Cians**, where the river plunges 1,600m (5,250ft) as it flows into the Var.

⊙ LE TRAIN DES PIGNES

The best way to explore the Nice backcountry is by car, but you can also take the Train des Pignes (www.trainprovence.com) to towns such as La Vésubie, Puget-Theniers, Entrevaux and St-André-des-Alpes. The one-metre narrow-gauge railway was a spectacular engineering feat when it was built in the 1890s. There are four return trips a day between the Gare de Provence in Nice and the spa town of Digne-les-Bains. Vintage steam trains run between Puget and Annot (May–June and Sept–Oct) or Villars-sur-Var (July–Aug) on Sunday (tel: 04 97 03 80 80).

Another spectacular excursion is to the Vésubie Valley, with its mountain slopes and rushing waters. Visit **Saint-Martin-Vésubie**, on a spur between two torrential streams. At the Mercantour National Park, don't miss the **Vallée des Merveilles** (June–Oct) with its prehistoric rock engravings.

The sinuous road leading up to the Madone d'Utelle, at 1,174m (3,850ft), passes by an 18th-century church in **Utelle**. At the summit you'll find a breathtaking view and a sanctuary founded in AD850 (rebuilt in 1806).

THE CORNICHES

The pre-Alpine mountains drop down to the sea between Nice and Menton, creating some spectacular scenery as they do so.

The highest views are from the route known as the Grande Corniche, built by Napoleon along the ancient Aurelian Way. The Moyenne (middle) Corniche offers a vivid contrast between cliffs and sea. The Corniche Inférieure (lower), or Corniche du Littoral, runs beside the sea and can be crowded in summer, but does include some worthwhile places to visit.

CORNICHE INFÉRIEURE

Villefranche-sur-Mer ❷, 6km (4 miles) east of Nice, is one of the most sheltered Mediterranean harbours. Clinging to a steep slope under the road, Villefranche offers instant charm, with its yellow, pink and red stucco or brick houses packed against the hill, its plunging alleyways and staircases and the covered **rue Obscure** that snakes down to the sea. The quayside cafés are well placed for watching pleasure boats and for a view of Cap Ferrat, pointing off to the left like a green finger.

On the right, below the town's old citadel (built for the duke of Savoy in 1560), is the 14th-century Chapelle St-Pierre

(Wed–Mon 10am–noon, 3–7pm, closed 15 Nov–15 Dec), also known as the **Cocteau chapel**, since writer-artist Jean Cocteau decorated it in 1956. The bold pastel drawings completely fill the small vaulted chapel with scenes of fishermen and biblical episodes from the life of St Peter.

Further on lies the rocky peninsula of **Cap Ferrat ❸**. A short drive around will convince you that the rich really do appreciate privacy. The view is mostly of gates that hint of grandeur. The vast, cream-coloured villa that belonged to Leopold II of the Belgians can only be seen from afar. Somerset Maugham lived in Villa Mauresque, also rather well hidden. Microsoft co-founder Paul Allen owns the grand Villa Maryland, tucked away down a lane off avenue Denis Semeria.

One of the most palatial residences of all is the **Villa Ephrussi de Rothschild** (www.villa-ephrussi.com; mid-Feb–Oct daily 10am–6pm, July–Aug until 7pm, Nov–mid-Feb Mon–Fri 2–6pm, Sat–Sun 10am–6pm). Built between 1905 and 1912 by Béatrice Ephrussi, née Rothschild, the Italian-style villa is the delirious assemblage of an insatiable art collector. While you'll admire a Coromandel screen and other beautiful chinoiseries, as well as examples of Renaissance Louis XIII furniture and a few

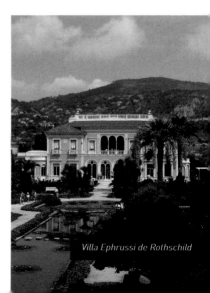

Villa Ephrussi de Rothschild

Impressionist paintings, the Rothschild Foundation shines in its collection of French 18th-century furniture, tapestries and Sèvres and Vincennes porcelain. The upper floor can be seen only on guided tours.

The themed gardens outside are perhaps the greatest attraction. Here you'll find a French formal garden with musical fountains, a Japanese garden with gravel and little shrines, exotic cacti, Provençal flora, an Italian Renaissance garden, and the romantic lapidary garden with its fragments of Gothic architecture and medieval statuary.

St-Jean-Cap-Ferrat is the port side of the peninsula, with a modern seaside promenade and an older fishing village; Jean Cocteau decorated the marriage room of its small town hall. A short stroll south from the port is Paloma Beach (www.paloma-beach.com), one of the loveliest and most exclusive private beaches on the French Riviera; there is an adjoining public beach.

Accessible from Cap Ferrat by the promenade Maurice Rouvier and only a ten-minute seaside walk away, **Beaulieu-sur-Mer** ❹ is an elegant town enjoying one of the mildest climates of the entire coast. There is a bustling fruit-and-vegetable market every morning in the main square, and popular quayside bars and restaurants surround the resort's marina.

Of particular interest is **Villa Kérylos** (www.villakerylos.com; Feb–Oct daily 10am–6pm, July–Aug until 7pm, Nov–Jan Mon–Fri 2–6pm, Sat–Sun and school holidays 10am–6pm), one of the few great villas on the Riviera open to the public. Built by scholar-musician-bibliophile Théodore Reinach in the early 20th century, it is a painstaking replica of an idealised Greek villa, constructed from marble, alabaster and exotic woods. Ancient Greek antiques, including vases, statuettes and mosaics, have been incorporated into the overall design.

GRANDE CORNICHE

The **Grande Corniche** road goes all the way to Menton, via Roquebrune. You can stop off at **La Turbie**, or explore inland villages such as Peillon and Peille (see page 42).

La Turbie's star attraction is the **Trophée des Alpes**, a ruin standing guard over Monaco. Emperor Augustus built it in 6BC to celebrate victory over various peoples who had prevented the construction of a road between Rome and Gaul.

MOYENNE CORNICHE

One highlight of the **Moyenne Corniche** (the best road of the three) is the 'perched' village of **Eze ❺**, hanging at a gravity-defying angle above the sea – which is majestic and deep blue from this perspective. Views from here rate as among the most

View over Eze village

Narrow streets of Roquebrune

magnificent on the coast. Medieval Eze is closed to traffic but not to tourists, who flock here in all seasons, ambling around the tiny stone streets filled with souvenir shops. On the site of an old château, demolished in 1706 by Louis XIV, is the garden **Le Jardin Exotique** (www.jardinexotique-eze.fr; daily Jan–Mar and Nov–Dec 9am–4.30pm, April–June and Oct 9am–6.30pm, July–Sept 9am–7.30pm), full of exotic flowers and cacti.

Further on, the Moyenne Corniche skirts Monaco (see page 43). Enjoy the stunning view at **Cabbé** before turning off for **Roquebrune Village**. Instead of Roquebrune (literally, 'brown rock'), the town should really have been called 'Roquerose' – since, on a sunny day, pink is the overriding colour here, because of the reflections from the sienna-red buildings along the streets. You can visit the keep of the **castle** (daily June–Sept 10am–1pm, 2.30–7pm, Feb–May 10am–12.30pm, 2–6pm, Oct–Jan until 5pm), built in the 10th century by the count of Ventimiglia to fend off the

Saracens. Stony and spartan, the ruin still looks very much the fortress, with walls around 2–3.5m (6–12ft) thick.

Part of the Roquebrune municipality, the **Cap Martin** promontory is a millionaires' enclave, green with pine and olive trees, and favoured in the 19th century when sea-bathing was not in vogue.

MENTON

Hot spot of the French Riviera for climate, **Menton** ❻ is especially appreciated by retired people because of its warmth, slow pace of life, casinos and long seaside promenade.

Lemons flourish here and in February there is a festival dedicated to the crop (see page 102). A long pebble beach and the promenade George V lead to a 16th-century bastion on the harbour, now the **Musée du Bastion** (Wed–Mon 10am–6pm), decorated with pebble mosaics and ceramics by the artist-poet Jean Cocteau who was a regular visitor to the town in the 1950s.

Cocteau also painted the bold allegorical frescoes that adorn the town hall's **Salle des Mariages** (place Ardoïno; Mon–Fri 8.30am–noon, 2–4.30pm). In 2011, the new **Musée Jean Cocteau Collection Séverin Wunderman** opened (2 quai Monléon; www.museecocteaumenton.fr; Wed–Mon 10am–6pm), to showcase a donation from a private collector of 1,800 works by the artist and some of his famous contemporaries. The striking modern building was designed by the award-winning French architect Rudy Ricciotti who is based west along the coast in Bandol and who is also responsible for the new Département des Arts de l'Islam at the Musée du Louvre in Paris. Next to the collection is the covered **Halles**, which has an excellent food market every morning. From nearby place aux Herbes you can head uphill to reach the heart of the Italianate **vieille ville** (old town). Here the 17th-century **Basilique St-Michel Archange** (daily 10am–noon, 3–5pm, closed Sat–Sun am) occupies a delightful square with

Serre de la Madone garden

a view across to Italy. You can also reach the church from the quays by steps decorated with patterns in black and white pebbles. The parvis in front of the church is used for concerts each summer during the Festival de Musique de Menton, one of the Riviera's oldest music festivals.

Across the square stands a second baroque church, the **Chapelle de la Conception**. At the top of the hill with views over the old town and the bay, the **Cimetière du Vieux-Château**, built where the castle once stood, contains the tombs of many of the Russian and British families who settled here from the end of the 19th century, including that of William Webb Ellis, creator of the modern game of rugby.

Back on the main road towards Roquebrune, the pink and white **Palais Carnolès** (Wed–Mon 10am–noon, 2–6pm) contains a fine art museum and is set amid a garden of citrus trees.

Indeed, Menton's mild climate has made the town a paradise for gardeners who introduced all sorts of Mediterranean, tropical and subtropical species. Two gardens are easily accessible to the public. The **Jardin Botanique Exotique du Val Rahmeh** (avenue Saint-Jacques; Wed–Mon Apr–Sept 9.30am–12.30pm, 2–6pm; Oct–Mar 10am–12.30pm, 2–5pm), arranged around a 1920s villa, proves that everything can grow in Menton, as a winding trail leads between magical and medicinal plants, towering palms, tropical ferns, and exotic cocoa, fruit and spice trees. The **Serre de la Madone** (route de Gorbio; www.serredelamadone.com; Tue–Sun Jan–Mar 10am–5pm, Apr–Oct until 6pm) is a romantic garden designed in the 1920s with pools, terraces, fountains and statues by Lawrence Johnson, creator of the garden at Hidcote Manor in England.

MENTON EXCURSIONS

Around Menton, hikers can venture up through groves of gnarled olive trees, pine and scrub oak and, finally, thick *maquis* scented with aromatic wild herbs.

A worthwhile inland excursion from Menton is a winding 15km (9 mile) road up into the mountains as far as **Sospel**, a small Alpine town of great charm on the banks of the River Bévêra. This was the second most important town in the old Comté of Nice, and although parts were badly bombed during World War II, the old medieval town, with its arcaded streets and gaily painted houses, remains intact.

Sights include the 13th-century **church of St-Michel** and an 11th-century bridge (restored in 1953), which still has its old **tollgate** in the middle, now home to the tourist office.

There is excellent walking in the area; full details

Sospel on the River Bévêra

are available from the tourist office (tel: 04 93 04 15 80). You can also visit Sospel by train from Nice station. The journey takes just over an hour, and the train continues onwards to the mountain town of Tende, then passes through a tunnel at the Col de Tende at 1,900m (6,232ft), before reaching Cuneo in Italy.

For a full day out, you could continue north to **Col du Turini**, on the edge of the Parc National du Mercantour, a pass at 1,600m (5,248ft) with some exceptional flora and stunning forested mountain scenery, plus a couple of hotel-restaurants. (Do take a jumper, as it is chilly, even in midsummer.) Then head south for a memorable drive via **Peïra-Cava** – a village (good for skiing in winter) perched on a rocky outcrop between the valleys of the Bévêra and the Vésubie. Just outside the village, look for a sign to **La Pierre Plate**, where there is a stone orientation table and wonderful views as far as the islands off the Cannes coast.

The road then passes the medieval villages of **Lucéram**, **L'Escarène** (on the old salt route from Nice to Turin) and **Peillon**, with superb 15th-century frescoes in the Chapelle des Pénitants Blancs. Return to the coast via the historic old town of **Peille** and the fortified village of **Sainte-Agnès**, which is claimed to be the highest of the local perched villages.

The perched village of Peillon

Look out, too, for **L'Annonciade**, a Capuchin monastery with a beautiful view, and the picturesque medieval towns of **Gorbio** and **Castellar**.

If you long for a taste of some real Italian spaghetti, just cross the border to **Ventimiglia**. A visit here should include the Romanesque cathedral, the 11th-century baptistery and if possible the Friday street market. It is easier to travel by train than to try to park in the town.

Monaco

MONACO

This fairytale princedom with its population of over 38,000, an enclave rising from the rocks above the sea, is famed for its casino and its wealth (residents pay no income tax). **Monaco** ❼ owes much of its current success to the late Prince Rainier. The atmosphere here is both big-city and miniature operatic. This is a crowded paradise, with a population density comparable to that of Hong Kong, and cars jamming thoroughfares over the hills (use the public lifts, which take passengers up effortlessly).

Gambling is not the only attraction; a mere five percent of Monaco's revenue comes from the casino. Many other activities take precedence. For one thing, Monaco has a top European orchestra and ballet company, an opera house and a music festival. Then there are the motor rally and **Grand Prix**, which set the streets roaring. Monaco holds an international circus festival, flower show and TV festival, and also has a football team and a radio station that beams all over Europe. Last but not least, philatelists have long admired the principality's beautiful stamps.

In brief, Monaco refers to the whole principality and geographically the historic peninsula-rock (the principality is often referred to as 'le Rocher'); glamorous Monte Carlo (Mt Charles) is the newer 19th-century area that curves out east of the rock. In between lies La Condamine, a landfill flat area, comprising the harbour and modern business district. A fourth district, Fontvieille, is a new town built on reclaimed land to the west, while Larvotto is the beach area to the east.

MONTE CARLO

All roads lead to the main **Casino A** (www.montecarlocasinos. com; daily guided tours 9am–noon; gaming rooms open from 2pm: smart dress and ID required) and **Opéra** (www.opera.mc), introduced by a neatly tended garden-promenade. Any resemblance to the Paris Opéra Garnier is more than coincidental since architect Charles Garnier designed both.

A lavish foyer, full of frescoes and voluptuous caryatids in 19th-century style, takes you into the Opéra. Off to the left are the gambling rooms – if you can tear your eyes away from the roulette wheels, the ornate décor here is a sheer delight.

Next door is the lively **Café de Paris**, a popular rendezvous that hums with the whir of slot machines, helpfully installed for the use of gambling fans between drinks. Across the square stands the **Hôtel de Paris**, another opulent historical monument. Louis XIV's bronze horse in the entrance hall has so often been stroked for luck by gamblers that its extended fetlock shines like gold. The dining room has been brilliantly

Monte Carlo's Casino

redecorated in Louis XV style and was the first restaurant in Monaco to be awarded three Michelin stars (see page 109).

Down by the shore on avenue Princesse Grace, Villa Sauber is one of two beautiful *belle époque* villas (the other is Villa Paloma near the Jardin Exotique) that house the **Nouveau Musée National de Monaco** Ⓑ (www.nmnm.mc; daily 10am–6pm; free on Sundays), which aims to showcase the princi-pality's cultural heritage in a contemporary manner. This part of the museum hosts temporary exhibitions relating to art and entertainment alongside its permanent collection of art-works, theatre sets and costumes. Almost opposite is a mod-ern Japanese garden and the angular, glass-sided **Grimaldi Forum** (www.grimaldiforum.com), used for congresses, art exhibitions, concerts and ballet. A short walk east of here is Larvotto Beach, a mix of public and private beaches created from imported sand and lined with bars and restaurants.

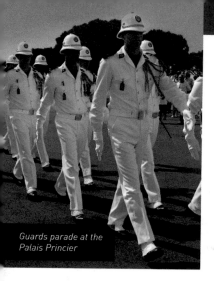

Guards parade at the Palais Princier

LE ROCHER

A short ride up the hill from the centre of town you'll find the **Palais Princier** ⓒ (www.palais.mc; daily Apr–mid-Oct 10am–6pm, Jul–Aug until 7pm; bus or taxi recommended as parking is limited), where Monaco's ruling family, the Grimaldis, live. The tour of the state apartments includes the magnificent 17th-century interior courtyard with its marble staircase, where Prince Albert married Charlene Wittstock in July 2011, and painted gallery, the **Galerie d'Hercule**. There are several rooms containing priceless antiques, paintings by Van Loo, Brueghel and Titian, a gallery of mirrors, royal family portraits, and the elaborate bed in which the Duke of York died in 1767. Year-round, at 11.55am, you can watch the changing of the guard outside the palace.

The **vieille ville** (old town) is also located on the Rock of Monaco. Along the narrow pedestrian streets riddled with souvenir shops, restaurants and other tourist attractions, a lively atmosphere prevails, ringing with the Italian inflections of Monégasque patois.

The neo-Romanesque **cathedral** (daily 8.30am–7pm), on rue de l'Eglise, contains a triptych by Louis Bréa in the right transept. Behind the high altar is the burial place of Princess Grace, who died in a road accident on the Corniche in 1982; Prince Rainier III, who died in 2005, has been buried alongside his beloved wife.

The **Musée Océanographique** on avenue St-Martin (www.
oceano.mc; daily Oct–Mar 10am–6pm, Apr–Sept 9.30am–7pm,
July–Aug until 8pm) is a formidable, grey-pillared construction, founded in 1910 by Prince Albert I, who spent the better
part of his time at sea. It was more recently directed by the
late Commandant Jacques-Yves Cousteau, the underwater
explorer. In the basement aquarium, playful sea lions, jaded
turtles and thousands of small incandescent fish cavort.

The **Jardin Exotique D** (www.jardin-exotique.mc; daily Feb–
Apr and Oct 9am–6pm, May–Sep 9am–7pm, Nov–Jan 9am–5pm)
above the area of La Condamine is worth visiting for its excellent view of the principality (take the lift from the port). Stepping
stones lead you through a display of exotic plants, including
fierce-looking spiny cacti in thousands of varieties from South

Monaco's cathedral

America and Africa. The 250 steps leading down to the Grotte de l'Observatoire (caves) will reward you with a cool promenade through crystal-clear stalactites and stalagmites. Nearby, **Villa Paloma** Ⓔ, the other location of the Nouveau Musée National de Monaco (56 boulevard du Jardin Exotique; www.nmnm.mc; daily 10am–6pm; free on Sundays), hosts temporary exhibitions around modern art, design and architecture.

Ⓞ THE GRIMALDIS

The Rock of Monaco has been inhabited since the Stone Age. In 1215, the Genoese built a fortress on it, and the Guelf and Ghibelline factions disputed it, until finally, in 1297, the Guelfs, led by François Grimaldi, gained the upper hand. The Grimaldi family has hung on tenaciously ever since.

Treaties with powerful neighbours assured Monaco's independence over the years (except for a French interlude from 1793 to 1814). Roquebrune and Menton broke off from the principality in 1848 and were later bought by France. Looking for a new source of revenue, Monaco's ruler Charles III founded the Société des Bains de Mer (still owner of the principality's grandest hotels, restaurants and casinos) in 1861 to operate gambling facilities. The casino, opera house and hotels were built, and a railway line was extended to Monaco.

In spite of legal tangles, Monaco has retained its independent (and tax-free) status, with open boundaries to France. It has its own international phone code, however; dial 00 377 if calling here from France.

Monaco is a pleasant place to live, but it's almost impossible to become a citizen – unless you can find some Monégasque ancestors.

A little way off in Fontvieille the **Princess Grace Rose Garden** has 150 different varieties of the sweet-smelling blooms. There is also a zoo, which is small and friendly but unspectacular except for the good view, and the **Collection des Voitures Anciennes** (www. palais.mc; daily 10am–6pm), the princely collection of vintage cars.

Château-Musée Grimaldi

NICE TO CANNES

In all respects, the stretch between Nice and Cannes is one of the richest areas of the French Riviera. The scenery can be absolutely magnificent and artworks abound both along the coast and in the villages of the hinterland.

CAGNES-SUR-MER AND VILLENEUVE-LOUBET

Spread out over hills covered with orange and olive trees, **Cagnes-sur-Mer** ❽ comprises the seaside resort of **Cros-de-Cagnes**, the modern commercial section of **Le Logis**, and **Haut-de-Cagnes**, the ancient hill town crowned by a fortress, the prettiest and most interesting part of the trio. Narrow, cobbled streets corkscrew to the **Château-Musée Grimaldi** (Castle Museum; Wed–Mon May–Sept 10am–1pm, 2–6pm, Oct–Apr until 5pm). Enter by passing through an ivy-covered, oblique-angled patio with galleries all around and a huge pepper tree in the centre. On the ground floor of the castle is a curious museum devoted to the olive – its history, cultivation and literature – probably the greatest tribute ever paid to that fruit. Upstairs you'll find exhibits of contemporary art and a ceremonial hall with a 17th-century *trompe l'œil* ceiling, *The Fall of Phaethon*, by Genoese artist Giulio Benso Pietra. One extraordinary room contains 40 portraits of Suzy Solidor, the one-time cabaret queen, as seen by 20th-century painters – ranging from a doe-eyed girl wearing a sailor suit by Van Dongen to a raffish portrait of her in a matador's hat.

Continuing west along the coast, the somewhat downmarket resort of **Villeneuve-Loubet** is usually associated with the Marina Baie des Anges, a 1970s development that has become a local landmark, but, again, there is an older village 3km (2 miles) inland along the Loup River. Narrow streets climb up to the medieval **Château** (ask at the tourist office about guided tours, tel: 04 92 02 66 16), where François I and his court spent three weeks leading up to the signature of the Treaty of Nice in 1538. At the foot of the village the **Musée Escoffier de l'Art Culinaire** (Sept–Oct and Dec–June daily 2–6pm, July–Aug until 7pm as well as 10am–noon on Wed and Sat) honours the memory of Auguste Escoffier, 'king of chefs and chef of kings', in the house where he was born in 1846.

Musée Renoir

The artist Auguste Renoir spent his last years (1907–19) in his villa, Les Collettes, east of Cagnes. Now the Musée Renoir (winter Wed–Mon 10am–noon, 2–5pm, summer until 6pm), the building still feels like a private home. His studios are filled with memorabilia, and there is a small display of paintings, as well as the bronze sculptures he increasingly turned to at the end of his life.

St-Paul-de-Vence

ST-PAUL-DE-VENCE

St-Paul-de-Vence ❾ is another venerable bastion, built within spade-shaped walls and looming over what were once green terraces of vineyards and cypress trees – now a parade of elegant country villas in lush gardens. The walled feudal city, entered by foot under a tower and arch with a cannon pointing at you, was built by François I in the 16th century as a defence against Nice and the dukes of Savoy.

Just outside the gateway, under the big plane trees of **place du Général de Gaulle**, you'll usually find a lively game of *pétanque* (or *boules*), the archetypally French outdoor bowling game. The **Colombe d'Or hotel** (www.lacolombedor.com) across the street has an important private collection of modern art, acquired from Picasso, Léger and Calder in exchange for meals in the restaurant. Within the walls a tour of the narrow, tourist-thronged pedestrian streets takes only a few minutes,

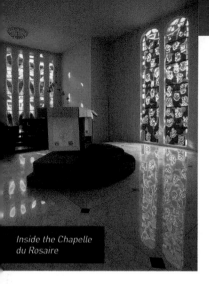

Inside the Chapelle du Rosaire

but take the time to stop at the Grande Fontaine and Gothic church.

On a wooded hill just outside St-Paul is one of the world's greatest modern art museums – the **Fondation Maeght** (www.fondation-maeght.com; daily July–Sept 10am–7pm, Apr–June until 6pm, Oct–Mar 10am–1pm and 2–6pm), inaugurated in 1964 by art dealer Aimé Maeght and his wife, Marguerite. The museum sits in a green grove of dark pines. Full of visual surprises, the brick and white-concrete construction designed by Spanish-American architect José Luis Sert is an ideal place for displaying modern art. The permanent collection, including paintings and lithographs by many of the great names of 20th-century art, is packed away in summer to make room for a temporary show. Throughout the year you can see sculptures and mosaics integrated into the building and surrounding garden, with many fine works by Braque, Miró and Giacometti.

VENCE

Vence ⑩ is an ancient bishopric with middle-age spread, as the lovely old city has been girdled by newer shops and houses. English and French artists and retirees all like the bustling atmosphere, the surrounding hills and the peace that falls at night (off-season, of course).

In the 17th century, Antoine Godeau became bishop of Vence. A society wit, he turned to holy orders at the age of 30, then undertook the restoration of the cathedral, founded new industries to give work to his parishioners and was appointed one of the first members of the Académie Française.

The best scenic points of old Vence are **place du Peyra**, with its gurgling fountain and friendly cafés, the **cathedral** and place du Frêne, with an ash tree whose trunk must be at least 2m (6ft) in diameter. Abutting a medieval tower on one side of the square,

⊙ MATISSE AND CHAGALL

Matisse (1869–1954) was born and brought up in the industrial north of France. He first visited St-Tropez in 1904 and was immediately seduced by the vibrant colours of the Mediterranean. His painting was transformed, characterised by the brilliance of his palette. From 1916 he spent part of every year working in Nice, and in 1921 bought an apartment in the old town, later moving to Cimiez. In 1949–51 he worked on the Chapelle du Rosaire (Chapel of the Rosary) at Vence – a gift to the Dominican nuns who cared for him during a long illness.

Marc Chagall (1889–1985) was born in Russia, studied art in St Petersburg and moved to Paris in 1910. Between the two world wars he worked on Old Testament book illustrations, which reveal clear evidence of his interest in Russian folk-painting. He became a French citizen in 1937; from 1949 until his death, he spent much time on the French Riviera at Vence, where he decorated the cathedral baptistery in 1979. His work is on permanent display at the Maeght Foundation (see page 52) and a major collection of biblical paintings is exhibited at Cimiez (see page 32).

On the beach at Antibes
looking towards Fort Carré

the **Château de Villeneuve-Fondation Emile Hugues** (Tue–Sun 10am–12.30pm, 2–6pm, closed between exhibitions), 17th-century baronial residence of the powerful Villeneuve family, is used for temporary exhibitions of modern and contemporary art.

Tourists often rush past Vence on their way to the **Chapelle du Rosaire** on the road to Saint-Jeannet (www.chapellematisse. com; Oct–Apr Tue, Thu, Fri 10am–12pm and 2–5pm, Wed and Sat 2–5pm, Apr–Oct until 6pm). Dedicated by Henri Matisse to the Dominican nuns who cared for him during a long illness, the chapel is the crowning achievement of the artist, who was in his eighties and practically blind when he completed it. The stained-glass windows in bold patterns of royal blue, bright green and yellow give radiant light to the simple chapel, two walls of which are decorated by powerful line-drawn figures on white faïence.

A short tour of the **Loup Valley** is worthwhile and will take you less than a day. Highlights include **Tourrettes-sur-Loup ⓫** (tourist office: 2 place de la Libération; tel: 04 93 24 18 93), a delightful old town popular with artisans and artists and famous for being the home of **Confiserie Florian** (Le Pont du Loup; www.confiserieflorian.co.uk; daily guided tours 9am–noon and 2–6pm), a family-run company that makes traditional sweets and jams using local fruit and flowers. The town is also well-known for growing violets, which are celebrated with a festival each March. There are also several waterfalls (Cascade de Courmes, Cascade des Demoiselles) in the area and the spectacularly sited village of **Gourdon** (tourist office: 24 rue de Majou; tel: 05 65 275252), built on a spur 758m (2,500ft) high. The valley offers plenty of opportunities for walking and cycling and the tourist offices will have route maps and details of bike hire.

ANTIBES AND JUAN-LES-PINS

Founded by the Phocaeans in the 4th century BC, lively **Antibes** ⑫ acquired its name (Antipolis – the 'city opposite') because it lay facing Nice across the Baie des Anges. The first landmark you'll see here is the imposing square fortress, **Fort Carré** (opening times vary, tel: 04 92 90 52 13 for details). This was the French kings' stronghold against the dukes of Savoy, who controlled Nice. In 1794, Napoleon lodged his family here while supervising the coastal defence, and was himself briefly imprisoned in the fort. As times were hard, his sisters filched figs and artichokes from neighbouring farmers. Today the hills around Antibes are lined with glassy greenhouses; flower-growing is the main local industry. Don't miss a tour around the ramparts, rebuilt by Louis XIV's chief engineer, Vauban, in the 17th century along the original medieval lines.

South of the harbour, the Château Grimaldi, now the **Musée Picasso** (Tue–Sun mid-June–mid-Sept 10am–6pm, mid-Sept–mid-June 10am–1pm, 2–6pm), is a white stone castle with a

Romanesque tower built by the lords of Antibes on a Roman site. In addition to several classical relics, the museum possesses a large Picasso collection. In 1946, when the artist was having difficulty finding a place to work, the director of Antibes' museum offered him the premises as a studio. Picasso set to work among the dusty antiquities. Inspired by his surroundings, he completed over 145 works in a period of six months. The grateful artist donated these drawings, ceramics and paintings to the museum, highlights of a collection that also includes works by Hartung, Balthus and de Stael, and sculptures by Germaine Richier on the terrace.

Next to the château-museum is a 17th-century church, L'Eglise de l'Immaculée Conception, with a Romanesque apse and transept and an altarpiece attributed to Louis Bréa. Behind the square you'll find a maze of old streets and the **covered market** (cours Masséna, daily 6am–1pm, closed Mon Sept–May), which sells food in the morning and arts and crafts from 3pm (mid-June–Sept Tue–Sun, Sept–mid-June Fri–Sun).

Just around the bay lies the **Cap d'Antibes**, a quiet, pine-covered peninsula with a wealth of big, beautiful houses and a venerable hotel, the Hôtel du Cap-Eden-Roc. It once served as a model for F. Scott Fitzgerald; today, it is popular with film stars and magnates, who can sometimes be seen lolling around its pool poised high above the sea.

An historic villa that can be visited is the **Villa Eilen Roc** (Wed and 1st and 3rd Sat of each month 2–5pm), designed by Charles Garnier of Paris and Monte Carlo opera houses fame; its palm-tree-filled gardens provide the stage for the Musiques au Cœur festival in July. On the east of the cape, the long, sandy **Plage de la Garoupe** has a mixture of private beaches and public stretches.

The **Chapelle de la Garoupe** houses **Notre-Dame-de-la-Garde** and **Notre-Dame-du-Bon-Port** (chemin du Calvaire,

Sat–Thu 11am–4.30pm Fri 2.30–4.30pm), which is of curious composition: one nave is 13th-century, the other 16th, and each is dedicated to a different Madonna. They are both filled with ex-votos, all kinds of naïve art works or objects offered as prayers of thanks to the Madonna. There are great views over the coast from here.

Glass-maker in Biot

Around the western side of the cape is the sandy, crescent-shaped bay of **Juan-les-Pins**. The resort enjoyed its heyday in the 1920s and 1930s, after American tycoon Frank Jay Gould built a big hotel and casino in a pinewood setting there. Sleepy in winter, the town becomes rather wild in summer, with a brash atmosphere generated by a host of nightclubs, cafés, boutiques spilling their wares onto the streets and a restless, fun-seeking crowd of young people.

VALLAURIS AND BIOT

The artisans' towns of Vallauris and Biot are only a few minutes' drive from Antibes. **Vallauris** ⑬ is inevitably associated with Picasso, who worked here from 1948 until 1955. He presented the town with the bronze statue *L'homme au Mouton* (Man with a Sheep) – on place du Marché – and decorated the Romanesque chapel inside the château, now the **Musée National Picasso 'La Guerre et la Paix'** (Château de Vallauris, place de la Libération;

July–Aug daily 10am–12.45pm and 2.15–6.15pm, Sept–June Wed–Mon 10am–12.15pm, 2–5pm), with the mural *War and Peace*. The château – a largely Renaissance building constructed over an earlier abbey – also contains the **Musée Magnelli** (same hours), with paintings by Italian-born artist Alberto Magnelli, and the **Musée de la Céramique** (same hours). The latter traces the town's pottery heritage from domestic wares, through the birth of art pottery with the Massier dynasty in the late 19th century, to modern art pottery. In 1946, Picasso met Georges and Suzanne Ramié of the Atelier Madoura, and began inventing his own wonderfully witty jugs, vases and plates, reviving a pottery industry that was in decline. Although marred by urban sprawl, Vallauris keeps the pottery tradition alive with numerous workshops lining the main street and the Biennale Internationale de la Céramique every two years.

Perched on a cone-shaped hill, the town of **Biot** ⑭ also bulges with craft shops and has a restored Romanesque church (too dark most of the time to see a fine Bréa altarpiece) and a colourful 13th-century square with fountains and arcades. Down the hill, in the Biot glassworks (www.verreriebiot.com; summer Mon–Sat 9.30am–8pm, Sun 10.30am–1.30pm and 2.30–7.30pm, winter, Mon–Sat until 6pm, Sun until 6.30pm), it is possible to watch craftsmen fashioning goblets and bowls from the heavy, tinted glass with minute bubbles for which the town is known.

Beside Biot, the **Musée National Fernand-Léger** (Wed–Mon May–Oct

Marineland

The dolphin and whale shows and shark-viewing tunnel at Marineland (www.marineland.fr; see page 94), near Biot railway station, are a hit with kids; also on the complex are an aquatic fun park, cowboy-themed children's farm and crazy golf.

10am–6pm, Nov–Apr
10am–5pm) stands out for
miles with its bold façade.
Light and airy inside, the
modern structure, built
and donated to France by
the artist's widow, houses
an incomparable collec-
tion of Léger's works,
including paintings and
huge tapestries.

GRASSE

Perfume capital of the
world, you can't miss the
enormous signs inviting

Musée National Fernand-Léger

you to visit the factories in **Grasse** ⓯. Although the Grassois
were distilling essential essences from local flowers as long
ago as the 13th century, the industry didn't bloom until the
Italian Medici family launched the fashion of scented gloves
in the 16th century (Grasse was also a centre of glove production). Today the town is an industrial centre rather than a
tourist one, also making the scents and flavourings that go into
countless toiletries, foods and household cleaning products.

Hairpin bends climb up a steep hill to the casino and the
Musée International de la Parfumerie (boulevard du Jeu de
Ballon; www.museesdegrasse.com; May–Sept daily 10am–
7pm, Oct–Mar Wed–Mon 11am–6pm, Apr daily 11am–6pm),
where the history and manufacture of perfume are explained.
Nearby, the **Musée d'Art et d'Histoire de Provence** (rue
Mirabeau; www.museesdegrasse.com; May–Sept daily
10am–7pm, Oct–Apr 10am–5.30pm) is housed in an elegant

Inside Parfumerie
Fragonard, Grasse

18th-century mansion that was once owned by the marquise de Cabris. The original furniture remains in remarkably good condition; among the less conventional and intriguing items on display, look out for a pewter bathtub on wheels and a carved wooden bidet-chair with a shell-shaped basin. Between the two museums is the small **Musée Provençal du Costume et du Bijou** (www.museesde-grasse.com; daily 10am–1pm, 2–6pm), a collection of 18th- and 19th-century regional costumes and jewellery.

From here rue Jean Ossola leads deep into the old town, with its crooked streets, small squares and fountains. Inside the sober, ochre-stone **cathedral**, begun in the 12th century and restored in the 17th, you'll find cradle-vaulting and a rare religious canvas by Jean-Honoré Fragonard, *Le Lavement des Pieds* (The Washing of the Feet).

The most charming spot in town is the friendly, crowded **place aux Aires**, with its fountains, arcades and sculptured 18th-century façades. The morning market is a palette of colours (flowers and vegetables) under the blue shade of lotus and plane trees.

The **Villa-Musée Jean-Honoré Fragonard** (www.fragonard. com; May–Sept daily 10am–7pm, Oct–Apr Wed–Mon 11am–6pm; guided tours only), located on boulevard Fragonard, occupies the villa where the artist spent a year to escape the French Revolution. He arrived with a series of paintings, depicting love scenes, all of which had been turned down in Paris by Madame du Barry. The majority of the series is now in the Frick Museum in New York, but the excellent and sensuous *Les Trois Grâces (The Three Graces)* remains here.

⊙ THE SCENT OF GRASSE

Three perfume manufacturers, Fragonard (www.fragonard. com), Galimard (www.galimard.com) and Molinard (www. molinard.com) – note that all three are outside the town centre – offer factory tours in several languages, giving an insight into the various complicated processes of distillation, *enfleurage* and chemical extraction that go into making perfume essences, and the art of 'the nose' in composing new fragrances. They also offer perfume initiation courses where visitors can create their own eau de toilette with the help of a master perfumer.

The manufacturers use at least 10,000 tonnes of flowers – violets (from January to March), mimosa (February), daffodil (April), rose, orange-flowers, etc – in order to produce their essence. The gleaming brass cauldrons, alembics and other trappings displayed in the factories, although mainly for show, do give an idea of the first steps in making perfume and soap. The high price of perfume becomes understandable when you realise it takes a tonne of petals to produce just 1kg (2lb) of essence. Nowadays many of the raw ingredients are imported; others such as musk and amber-grey formerly made from animals are chemically synthesised, but Grasse's expertise keeps it at the forefront of the industry.

CONTINUING INLAND

Grasse is a good starting point for side trips. Gourdon and the Loup Valley (see page 54) are off to the northeast; to the southwest are the Tanneron range and the man-made lake of Saint-Cassien, a popular place for windsurfing.

Cabris (6km/4 miles from Grasse on the D4 road) commands an impressive view from its château ruins. Another 8km (5 miles) or so further on, the **Grottes de St-Cézaire** (grottoes) provide a refreshing respite from the sun, with stalactite shapes in dark red and pink. As for **St-Cézaire** itself, it's a quiet, pretty town with a Romanesque chapel and pleasant views.

You can continue north through wild, rocky limestone hills with low trees and bushes, up to **Mons** (32km/20 miles from Grasse), an ancient perched village, to the **Col de Valferrière**, and back down the Route Napoléon (the RN85) through **Saint-Vallier-de-Thiey** and some splendid panoramas.

Alternatively, you may want to continue west into the Var, visiting towns such as **Fayence** (27km/17 miles from Grasse),

☉ CANNES IS 'DISCOVERED'

Cannes was just a quiet fishing village in 1834 when Lord Brougham, a leading English law reformer, had to stop over on his way to Italy because of a cholera epidemic. This chance visit turned out to be longer than expected: he built a home and returned every winter for the rest of his life. A champion of his city, Lord Brougham prodded Louis-Philippe of France to provide funds for a jetty below the old town. Many English aristocrats followed Brougham to Cannes, swelling the local population. A handsome statue of Brougham presides over square Prosper Mérimée, across from the Palais des Festivals.

Bargemon (44km/27.5 miles) and **Draguignan** (some 56km/35 miles away), or perhaps the pink-stoned **Abbaye du Thoronet** (www.monuments-nationaux.fr), a two-hour drive from Grasse.

CANNES

During the film festival in May and the music industry fair (MIDEM) held in January, **Cannes**  (pop. around 75,000) loses its habitual cool. The rest of the year the city devotes itself to its tourist vocation – as an elegant, cosmopolitan resort in a splendid setting, boasting the liveliest pleasure port on the Riviera.

The history of Cannes is tied to the two islands you can see off the coast, the Lérins. On the smaller one, in the 4th century Saint Honorat founded a monastery, which became a shrine for pilgrims. In the 10th century the Count of Antibes gave the Cannes mainland to the Lérins monks, who built ramparts to defend their territory against incursions by Moorish pirates.

In 1815, Napoleon Bonaparte stopped in Cannes after landing at Golfe-Juan, but the inhabitants gave him such a chilly reception that he had to move on to Grasse.

LA CROISETTE

Like Nice's promenade des Anglais, **La Croisette** Ⓐ is a magnificent showcase, with gleaming hotels lining a flowered boulevard, and restaurants and private beach concessions taking up much of the stretch in summer. The golden sand of the beach along the promenade is mainly imported from Fréjus. At one end of La Croisette lies the old port and the **Palais des Festivals**; at the other, a second marina and the Palm Beach Casino. The film festival, plus numerous other events, are held in the Palais, which also contains a casino.

With their designer clothes and jewellery shops, La Croisette and the parallel **rue d'Antibes** are two of the coast's most glamorous shopping streets. For more down-to-earth purchases – such as T-shirts, sandals, mouth-watering sausages and pastries – head for rue Meynadier, or stock up for a picnic at the wonderful **Marché Forville ®** (Tue–Sun 7am–1pm), a covered food market just behind it.

OLD TOWN

Looking uphill from the old port in the evening, you have a vision of the ramparts of the old town, **Le Suquet ©**, glowing with orange lights against the dark purple sky. You'll also see the **Tour du Suquet**, a 22m (72ft) -high square watchtower built by the Lérins monks. It was destroyed during the Revolution, but later restored as a favour to local fishermen who petitioned for a tall, visible navigational point. Now the white stone clock tower is a Cannes trademark.

The centre of the old town is place de la Castre, a quiet, pine-shaded square. The 17th-century church here has several polychrome statues. The **Musée de la Castre** (Apr–June and Sept Tue–Sun 10am–1pm, 2–6pm, July–Aug daily 10am–7pm, Oct–Mar Tue–Sun 10am–1pm, 2–5pm) houses a quaintly eclectic collection of everything from an Egyptian mummy's hand to a Japanese warrior's costume and a South Pacific hut pole. All this is the gift of Dutchman Baron Lycklama, who is portrayed wearing an extraordinary oriental outfit. The view over Cannes from Le Suquet is superb.

ILES DE LÉRINS

One of Cannes' most refreshing diversions is an excursion to the islands. Boats leave frequently in the summer from quai Laubeuf in front of the Radisson Blu 1835. The trip to Ste-Marguerite takes about 15 minutes, and about 30 minutes to St-Honorat; the islands stage sound-and-light shows during the season.

Cannes' Marché Forville

Closer to Cannes and the larger of the two islands is **Ste-Marguerite**, consisting of 2.5km (1.5 miles) of wooded hills, a minute 'main' street lined with fishermen's houses and a couple of restaurants. The island is named after Saint Honorat's sister, who founded her own religious order here. You can walk for hours among cool, fragrant woods and a grove of enormous eucalyptus trees.

Walk uphill to visit the 17th-century **Fort-Royal**, built under Cardinal Richelieu, and enjoy a superb view of Cannes, Antibes and the hills. The main attraction here is the dank and smelly prison of the 'Man in the Iron Mask', whose identity has been hotly contested. Between 1687 and 1698, a mysterious prisoner was kept in Fort-Royal. He wore a mask of cloth, not of iron, but was never allowed to take it off, and nobody knows for sure who he was or why he was imprisoned. One theory identifies him as an illegitimate brother of Louis XIV; another as the larcenous ex-finance minister of the Sun King, Fouquet. There's nothing to see but chains, faded ochre stone and modern graffiti, but the legend is intriguing.

The fort houses the **Musée de la Mer** (June–Sept daily 10am–5.45pm, Oct–Mar Tue–Sun 10am–1pm, 2–4pm, Apr–May until 5pm), which has artefacts salvaged from wrecks, including a ship from Roman times.

The island of **St-Honorat**, home of the monks who governed Cannes for nearly eight centuries, is once again a monastery, run by the Cistercian order. It is a peaceful retreat off-season with its pines, roses, lavender and the monks' vineyard. Several Romanesque chapels are scattered about.

The most striking construction on St-Honorat is the square, battlemented **château** – actually a fortified dungeon. Built in the 11th century over a Roman cistern, it served as a refuge for the monks during various attacks.

The 19th-century **monastery** (daily July–Sept, guided visits only) contains a small museum and church. Next door to the museum, the monks do a brisk trade in handicrafts, lavender scent and their own Lérina liqueur. There is a waterside restaurant and snack bar, La Tonnelle (www.tonnelle-abbaye-delerins.com), with lovely views back over the mainland.

CANNES' ENVIRONS

A soft backdrop of green hills characterises the countryside between Cannes and Grasse. Interesting stops include **Mougins** ⑰, a chic 15th-century fortified town (with some superb restaurants, see page 109); **Valbonne**, laid out on a grid plan, with a beautiful arcaded square shaded by elm trees and a brightly restored church; and **Plascassier**, a sleepy village perched on a hill.

THE ESTÉREL

Between Cannes and St-Raphaël lies a mass of porphyry rocks worn down and chipped by streams. This is the **Massif d'Estérel**, now not much more than 600m (2,000ft) at its highest (Mt Vinaigre), though the landscape is still abrupt and impressive. In spring, however, the scrub-herb hills are softened by the golden hue of mimosa. There are excellent possibilities for exploring the Estérel area by foot or bike (see page 91).

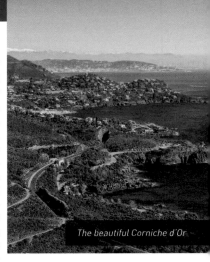

The beautiful Corniche d'Or

The original inland road here was the Aurelian Way, built by the eponymous Roman emperor during the 3rd century, but these days most people take the motorway running between Cannes and St-Raphaël.

CORNICHE D'OR

The motorway may be practical, but the coastal route – the **Corniche d'Or** (the Golden Corniche) – is much prettier. Red porphyry rocks tumble into the sea, making a jigsaw pattern of colours and shapes, tempting you to stop at every outcrop to admire the view or take a picture.

The coast's most glorious oddity, the **Château de la Napoule** (8km/5 miles west of Cannes; www.chateau-lanapoule.com; Feb–Nov daily 10am–6pm, guided tours 11.30am, 2.30pm, 3.30pm, 4.30pm, Nov–Feb weekends and school holidays

St-Raphaël's port

10am–5pm, guided tours 11.30am, 2.30pm, 3.30pm, weekdays 2–5pm, guided tours 2.30pm, 3.30pm), hovers in splendour over a tiny beach and harbour. Here, in 1919, American sculptor Henry Clews (scion of a wealthy New York family) restored the medieval château with towers and battlements, endowing every space with his own idiosyncratic artwork. Wildly imaginative, the sculptures range from a poignant Don Quixote to some pudgy grotesques. The rather eccentric Clews, who saw himself as a latter-day Quixote and his wife as 'The Virgin of La Mancha', filled his home with all kinds of mottoes ridiculing the 'aberrations' of society.

After **La Napoule** and then **Théoule**, with a château that served as a soap factory in the 18th century, you come to **Port-la-Galère**, a cascade of modern houses on a flowered, stony point. The Estérel is full of little resort towns with such euphonic names as **Le Trayas**, **Anthéor** and **Agay**. The Sémaphore du Dramont (a lookout for the coastguard), built on the ruins of a watchtower, offers sweeping views of the coast, and there is a marble monument near the road commemorating the American landing here on 15 August 1944.

The best time to see this stretch of coastline is at sunset, looking east, when colours and contrasts are most flamboyant – a Surrealist's dream.

ST-RAPHAËL

Booming **St-Raphaël**, an appealing resort built around a port for pleasure boats, acts as a focus for the whole Estérel area. The town's centre is a pleasant modern seafront (the old one was destroyed during World War II) with an ornamental fountain and pyramid commemorating Napoleon Bonaparte's debarkation after the 1799 Egyptian victories (see page 20).

In days gone by, there was a small holiday resort here for Roman legions based in nearby Fréjus. It stood more or less on the site of the present casino – if you can imagine the roulette tables replaced by tiled baths and fish ponds.

The 12th-century **Templars' church** in the old town (on rue des Templiers) is surmounted with a massive watchtower replacing the right-hand apse.

FRÉJUS

Little remains of the busy Roman naval town of **Fréjus** ⑱ (Forum Julii), founded in 49BC. The big harbour, built by Emperor Augustus into a great naval base and shipyard, has been completely filled up with silt deposits and replaced by modern Fréjus. A good part of the town was also rebuilt after the 1959 catastrophe, when a dam upstream over the River Reyran broke, killing over 400 people. At the mouth of the original Roman port is a new marina and apartment complex known as Port-Fréjus.

Fréjus

The town is still dotted with Roman vestiges. Most impressive is the **Arènes** (amphitheatre; Sun–Tue Apr–Sep 9.30am–12pm, 2–6pm, Jan–Mar and Oct–Dec until 4.30pm), a restored grey-green construction that once seated 10,000 spectators – nearly as large as the arenas of Arles and Nîmes. During the season, bullfights and music concerts are held here.

Other Roman ruins include a theatre and the massive reddish arches of the aqueduct that brought water in from the River Siagnole.

Nearly destroyed by the Saracens in the 10th century, the town was revived in 990 by Bishop Riculf, who established the fortified **Groupe Episcopal** (June–Sept daily 10am–12.30pm, 1–6.30pm, Oct–May Tue–Sun 10am–1pm, 2–5pm), a cathedral, dedicated to St-Léonce, and bishop's palace. Put your name down for a guided tour to see the carved Renaissance doors, the baptistery and the cloisters. One of the oldest religious buildings in France (late 4th–early 5th century), the **baptistery** is punctuated by black granite columns with Corinthian capitals from the ancient Fréjus forum. The original terracotta baptismal bowl was discovered in the course of archaeological research.

In the **cloister**, a double-deckered arcade surrounds a sweet-smelling garden of roses and cypress trees. The ceiling of the upstairs arcade is decorated with some amusing 14th-century creatures – imaginative scenes from the Apocalypse. The 10th-to 12th-century **cathedral**, with its 'broken cradle' vaulting, perfectly exemplifies the Early Gothic style of the region. It was built on the site of a Roman temple dedicated to Jupiter.

Nearby on place Calvini, the **Musée Archéologique** (Apr–Sept Tue–Sun 9.30am–12pm, 2–6pm, Oct–Mar Tue–Sat until 4.30pm) has a fine collection of Roman and early Ligurian tiles, mosaics and sculptures, including the two-faced bust of Hermes, looking in opposite directions, which is the town's symbol.

CÔTE DES MAURES

The Côte des Maures, culminating with the legendary resort of St-Tropez, is possibly the most exclusive stretch of the French Riviera. Inland, the Massif des Maures offers a welcome respite from the fray.

On the way to St-Tropez, you'll pass through the attractive town of **Ste-Maxime**, with a casino, a tiny beach and a wide promenade. This popular holiday resort, with its palm trees and esplanade, retains an appealing, almost Victorian atmosphere that is quite different from that of fashionable St-Tropez across the bay.

ST-TROPEZ

St-Tropez ⑲ barely manages to keep up with its glamorous reputation: celebrity escapades, the beauty of its little port, cafés filled with fashionable people, chic boutiques and scanty bikinis on nearby beaches.

Getting to St-Tropez

Traffic jams can make reaching St-Tropez a nightmare in high season. If you haven't got a yacht, get a good map and cut down the back roads from Ramatuelle or take the shuttle boat from Ste-Maxime.

In St-Tropez more than any other place on the French Riviera, you feel an unspoken desire to wear the right ensemble, be seen with the right people and show up in certain places at certain times of day or night. The atmosphere is enlivened by clusters of motorcycles roaring by, as well as haughty models and golden boys parading around. In winter it reverts to that of an easy-going fishing town.

The resort weathers its own snobbery while cultivating its legends. The name comes from a Roman Christian, Torpes, who was martyred in Pisa in AD68. The headless body, put adrift in a boat with a dog and a cockerel, came ashore in the Var region. You can see a tableau of the body drifting along with its animal companions in the local church, as well as a wide-eyed sculpture of the saint himself, surrounded with a lacy halo, his chest covered with heart-shaped medals.

The town was battered several times by the Saracens, and more recently by the German occupation and invasions of World War II, but the gallant little fishing village has always bounced back; it was renovated after the war with plans for modern urban development wisely rejected. In 1637 it routed a fleet of Spanish ships and still celebrates the victory in May with the **Bravade** (see page 95), a fête that also honours Saint Tropez himself. The locals get out their muskets, don 17th- and 18th-century costumes, and fire blanks in fun, noisy parades. (There is a similar, less important festival in mid-June.)

St-Tropez was first 'discovered' by the French writer Guy de Maupassant. In 1892, Paul Signac, a keen sailor, first stayed here and was soon followed by other artists, including Dufy, Matisse, Bonnard and, later, Dunoyer de Segonzac. In the 1920s, Colette wrote extensively at her villa here, La Treille

Quayside in St-Tropez

Muscate, but it was Roger Vadim's 1956 film *Et Dieu Créa la Femme*, starring Brigitte Bardot, that turned St-Trop into a jet-set destination.

The port

You can't miss the port with its restless crowds, vast gin-palace luxury yachts, often with uniformed crews, and pastel houses with pantiled roofs. Early-evening apéritif time is the moment to sit in the red director's chairs on the terrace of **Café Le Senequier** and watch the crowds parade by.

The **Musée de l'Annonciade** (Tue–Sun 10am–noon, 2–6pm), a former chapel situated on the west side of the port, houses an excellent collection of Impressionist and Post-Impressionist works. Many of the artists lived in and loved St-Tropez. You can view paintings by Signac, Van Dongen, Dufy, Bonnard and others in rooms lit by refracted St-Tropez sunshine. Outside, the quay space is crowded with contemporary artists, trying their best to sell their colourful works.

Old town

A short walk behind the quai Jean-Jaurès will take you to the **vieille ville** (old town) through an arcade by La Ponche (the old fishing port), past narrow old buildings now housing expensive hotels and boutiques, to the 17th-century **Citadelle** (daily Apr–Sept 10am–6.30pm, Oct–Mar 10am–12.30pm, 1–5.30pm). Situated on top of the hill, with its unusual hexagonal keep, it offers a fine view from the cannon-lined terrace. The moat, surrounded with greenery, provides living quarters for peacocks, ducks and some deer. The former Musée Naval de la Citadelle, now the **Musée de l'Histoire Maritime de St-Tropez**, contains souvenirs of a local hero, Admiral de Suffren (who took his fleet on an odyssey around the Cape of Good Hope in 1781), model

⊙ PLAGE DE PAMPELONNE

It's the Plage de Pampelonne that best maintains St-Tropez's reputation for sex, sea and sun: 5km (3 miles) of fine golden sand, stretching between Cap Pinet and Cap Camaret (and officially in the commune of Ramatuelle), bordered by pines and vineyards. Much of the territory is taken up by 'private' beach clubs, varying from the boho bamboo shack with its beach restaurant and sun loungers to designer haunts offering cosmopolitan menus, DJs and beauty treatments. Trendy spots include the veteran show-biz haunt Tahiti, venerable Club 55, Nikki Beach, Nioulargo, Key West and fish restaurant Chez Camille (www.chezcamille.fr), but there are also free public stretches where you can put up your parasol, and anyone can walk along the shorefront.

ships and diving equipment. West of here is the plane-tree-shaded place des Lices, which is full of local colour: a lively food market takes over on Tuesday and Saturday mornings, and games of *pétanque* provide the interest in the late afternoon.

Plage de Pampelonne

The beaches

St-Tropez is noted for its beaches. Nearby ones such as the **Plage des Graniers** and the **Bouillabaisse** are popular with locals on weekends, but many holiday visitors look down their noses at them. They go to **Les Salins** or the vast sandy crescent (9.5km/6 miles long) of **Pampelonne** that stretches in front of vineyards from Tahiti Beach to Cap Camarat.

Smooth-sanded and bordering a clear aquamarine sea, the beaches are fully equipped in summer with all manner of huts and shacks to furnish mattresses, umbrellas and sustenance to sunbathers. Part of the beach is traditionally given over to nudists. Every summer the beautiful people gravitate to the bar, restaurant or beach of the moment.

ST-TROPEZ PENINSULA AND THE MAURES

St-Tropez is surrounded by delightful spots to visit when you have had enough of the beach scene.

A short trip will take you up to the small historic hill towns of **Gassin** and **Ramatuelle** – with panoramic views and

Bird's-eye view of Port-Grimaud

pleasant restaurants – and the **Moulins de Paillas**, now fallen in ruins. They provide an introduction to the **Maures** mountains, the oldest geological mass of Provence: worn-down crystalline hills, deep green and covered with pines and scrub trees.

Heading north into the Maures over a long road full of hairpin bends through forests of chestnut and cork oak, you come to **La Garde-Freinet**. At 405m (1,328ft), the town is considerably cooler than the coast. It has an unspoilt charm that attracts crowd-weary Parisians and Brits. Its residents also make a living off the land – cork and chestnuts are major industries.

The ruins of an old fortress evoke the last stand of the marauding Saracens. For several centuries these pirates of Arab origin managed to hold out here as they pillaged the towns below, until they were thrown out in 973.

If you are pressed for time, head straight for **Grimaud**, at its best in the late afternoon, where you can look out to sea through Provençal lotus trees and enjoy a drink in a café. Grimaud was the fiefdom of Gibalin (Ghibelline) de Grimaldi. The fortress ruins lie in piles of stony remnants against a grassy hill. A sign warns of the danger of falling rocks, but you can take a look at the simple, barrel-vaulted 11th-century Templars' church (this is a restored version) and the arcaded charterhouse.

Port-Grimaud, 6.5km (4 miles) downhill on the bay of St-Tropez, is the modern French version of Venice. Designed by François Spoerry and opened in 1964, it is a series of artificial canals built on marshland, lined with houses and flowered terraces painted in the same cool pastel shades as St-Tropez.

Deep in the heart of the Maures, 25km (15 miles) west of Grimaud, **Collobrières** is an attractive village where the speciality is *marrons glacés* (sugared chestnuts). On the way, you might want to visit the **Chartreuse de la Verne** (Wed–Mon June–Aug 11am–6pm, Sept–May until 5pm, closed Jan and on days of high fire risk, tel: 04 94 48 08 00 to check), a Carthusian monastery on a remote hillside. Built out of local schist and green serpentine, the monastery, with its huge grain store, chapel and individual monks' cells, was founded in 1170 but abandoned after the French Revolution; it is now home to a community of nuns.

CORNICHE DES MAURES

For most French people, the Riviera stops at St-Tropez (some say St-Raphaël), but the coast continues. From La Croix Valmer, the Corniche des Maures (D559) runs through a string of resort towns. **Cavalaire** is an ungainly built-up sprawl, but **Le Rayol-Canadel** ⓴ has a beautiful flowered setting under the Maures hills and one of the most beautiful gardens on the coast. The **Domaine du Rayol** (www.domainedurayol.org; daily 9.30am–5.30pm, until 7.30pm in summer) creates different zones with Mediterranean climates, from Mexico and Chile to California and Australia, as well as the Mediterranean itself, against scintillating blue sea views.

Le Lavandou has suffered from urbanisation, though it's still very popular. The town has a lively beachside promenade and numerous restaurants. Uphill to the west is **Bormes-les-Mimosas**, a lovely retreat that lives up to its name – blooming not only with mimosa, but also oleander, roses, geraniums and bougainvillea. The town has a mass of narrow stepped streets and a lively café and restaurant scene in summer. Back down on the coast, Bormes' seaside suburb **La Favière** offers plenty of water sports. South of here the vineyard-covered **Cap de Brégancon** conceals several lovely beaches, including the **Plage de Cabasson**, under the eye of the closely guarded Fort de Brégancon (a presidential summer residence), and the **Plage de l'Estagnol**, a small curving sandy bay shaded by pine woods.

HYÈRES

Hyères 🉑 is the 'granny' of Mediterranean resorts. French holidaymakers were coming to this picturesque city, attracted by its mild climate, as early as the 18th century, even before the English started to winter in Nice. Queen Victoria occasionally chose to stay here on her visits to the French Riviera.

On place de la République, you'll see the 13th-century **church of St-Louis**, where Louis IX of France prayed after his return from a crusade in 1254; Hyères was the landing port for returning crusaders, though they disembarked at what is now the centre of town. Today, modern boulevards run right over the old harbour.

Bormes-les-Mimosas

Uphill market street rue Massillon (go in the morning when it's in full swing) brings you to place Massillon, home to restaurants, the Tour St-Blaise (an ancient Templars' building now used for exhibitions), and the Eglise Saint-Paul, a Gothic church renovated in the 16th century. Today Hyères' chief tourist attraction is the **Villa Noailles** (www.villanoailles-hyeres.com; Wed, Thu, Sat, Sun 1–6pm, Fri 3–8pm), located up the hill below the castle ruins. This masterpiece of early Modernist Cubist architecture was built in the 1920s by Robert Mallet-Stevens for avant-garde aristocrats Charles and Marie-Laure de Noailles, and restored in the 1990s for exhibitions. In its heyday it was an ultimate expression of modern living and aesthetics. Buñuel, Giacometti, Stravinsky and Man Ray were among the arty guests who lounged on its sun terraces or tried out newfangled exercise regimes in the pool and gym.

Jumble of rooftops in Hyères

Near the airport, the Giens Peninsula has long, sandy beaches and is a world-class spot for windsurfing.

ILES D'HYÈRES

Known as the Iles d'Or (Golden Isles) because of their mica-shot rocks – sometimes mistaken for gold – the Iles d'Hyères comprise three islands: Levant, Port-Cros and Porquerolles. The long, rocky **Ile du Levant** is France's nudist capital, where one of the first nudist colonies was established in the early 1930s – but you can, of course, also keep your trousers on. The eastern half of the island is off-limits as there is a naval base here.

Next to the Ile du Levant lies the **Ile de Port-Cros**, festooned with steep myrtle- and heather-decked hills and an abundance of bird life. This protected national park has its own population of flamingos, turtle doves, cormorants and puffins, as well as rare flowers, orchids and mushrooms when it's the season (mainly the tasty boletus and chanterelle varieties).

The largest island, **Porquerolles** ㉒, measuring 7 by 3km (4.5 by 2 miles), is another enchanting setting, much of it also a protected area, with lovely sandy beaches along its north shore (where the boat lands), vineyards and pine woods in the interior, and a southern shoreline of steep, rocky cliffs. There are numerous footpaths and the possibility of hiring bikes by the harbour.

Island ferries

TLV (tel: 04 94 58 21 81; www.tlv-tvm.com) runs ferries from Hyères to Port-Cros (1 hr) and Ile du Levant (1.5 hrs), and from Tour Fondue on the Presqu'Ile de Giens to Porquerolles (30 mins). Vedettes Iles d'Or (tel: 04 94 71 01 02; www.vedettesiles-dor.fr) go from Le Lavandou to Ile du Levant (35 mins; 1 hr via Port-Cros) and Porquerolles (40 mins).

TOULON

Toulon ㉓ is a major French naval port with a long history. Hidden behind the post-war housing blocks along **avenue de la République**, the pleasure port is a lively part of town, lined with popular cafés and brasseries. Several boat companies leave from here for trips around the bay (about one hour). The *Atlantes* sculpture by Puget, on the façade of the Mairie d'Honneur on quai Cronstadt, dates from the 17th century and is about all that's left of the old port. Another relic is the gateway to the arsenal, now the entrance to the **Musée National de la Marine** (place Monsenergue; www.musee-marine.fr; July–Aug daily 10am–6pm, Sept–June Wed–Mon, closed Jan).

Toulon

To the north are the remains of the **vieille ville** (old town). Head in this direction for place Puget, a gorgeous, typically Provençal square set just behind the ornate **Opéra de Toulon**, graced with a dolphin fountain and lots of greenery. Downhill is the narrow market street, rue d'Alger, a favourite for an evening stroll. Off to the left, the cathedral, **Sainte-Marie-de-la-Seds**, has a handsome baroque façade and 18th-century belfry. Another block east is cours Lafayette, one of the most animated indoor/outdoor market streets in Europe (Tue–Sun mornings). History enthusiasts can visit the nearby **Musée du Vieux-Toulon** at No. 69 (Tue–Sat 2–5.45pm).

Behind the old town, busy boulevard de Strasbourg forms the heart of 19th-century Toulon. On boulevard Maréchal Leclerc, the **Musée d'Art** (Tue–Sun noon–6pm) has works by the Provençal school and a collection of contemporary art. For glorious views over the coast, take the cable car to the top of Mont Faron where there is a zoo and a monument and museum dedicated to the Allied landings in 1944.

Shopping in the old streets of Antibes

WHAT TO DO

SHOPPING

Shopping is a delight on the French Riviera, with an enormous choice of merchandise. **Markets** (see page 84) and small individual shops remain an essential part of the French lifestyle, though very touristy locations, such as St-Paul-de-Vence and Mougins, have been taken over almost entirely by souvenir shops and arts-and-crafts galleries. All along the coast you will find plenty of **craft** workshops displaying a tempting array of top-quality original gifts with affordable price tags (for the most part).

Chic **boutiques** selling ultra-smart clothes and accessories at ultra-expensive prices abound in all the fashionable coastal resorts and large towns (try Le Métropole Shopping Center and avenue des Beaux-Arts in Monte Carlo, rue de France and rue de Paradis in Nice, rue d'Antibes and La Croisette in Cannes and anywhere in St-Tropez). You'll find all the usual French and international labels. Not surprisingly, most resorts also offer an excellent range of beachwear. For a local touch, Vilebrequin's flamboyantly printed men's swimming trunks (shops in St-Tropez, Cannes, Juan-les-Pins, Nice and Monte Carlo) and the strappy gladiator-style Tropézienne sandals made by Atelier Rondini since 1927 both originate in St-Tropez; the upmarket casualwear label Façonnable is based in Nice.

Food is a passion with the French, so there is no shortage of speciality shops in every village and town, where shopping for the delectable delicacies on display can be almost as much fun as eating them. For convenience-food shopping, small supermarkets are found everywhere except in the smallest villages.

Antiques, craft and produce markets are held throughout the region

MARKETS

The mild climate of the French Riviera makes shopping at open-air markets a pleasure, and few visitors can resist the profusion of colourful produce on display – abundant fresh fruit and vegetables, delicate farm-made cheeses, exotic Mediterranean fish, aromatic herbs, traditional Provençal fabrics and local arts and crafts. Market traders set up their stalls early: vans and trucks begin to arrive from 5am onwards, so parking may be at a premium. Some larger markets last all day, but most are over by 12.30pm. In summer some resorts have extra evening markets of crafts and regional produce. Here are a few favourites:

Antibes (old town): regional products every morning (except Monday Sept–May); craft market from 3pm (days/times vary, see page 56).

Cannes: general market and flower market every morning except Monday; antiques market on Saturday and Sunday.

Fréjus: general market Wednesday and Saturday morning.
Fréjus Plage: general market Tuesday and Friday in summer; crafts sold evenings in July and August.
Grasse: regional products market Saturday morning.
Hyères: general market Tuesday and Saturday.
Le Lavandou: food and general market Thursday morning.
Menton: covered market every morning; antiques and flea market every Friday.
Monaco: daily morning market.
Nice (cours Saleya): flower market Tue–Sun; regional products market every morning Tue–Sun; antiques sold on Monday.
Place Saint-François: fish market every morning Tue–Sun.
St-Tropez: general market Tuesday and Saturday morning.
Ste-Maxime: covered market Tuesday to Sunday (daily June–mid-Sept), outdoor market Thursday, crafts market every evening mid-June–mid-Sept.
Toulon (cours Lafayette): big food and general market, every morning Tue–Sun.
Vence: regional products Tuesday and Friday morning; antiques Wednesday.

WHAT TO BUY

Arts and crafts. Many talented artists and craftspeople work on the coast, drawn by the colourful landscape and wonderful light. *Foires artisanales* (craft fairs) are held throughout the summer, and in coastal resorts craft stalls are set up every evening during the summer. You will find painters, jewellers, potters, glass-blowers, wood-carvers, silk-screen painters and weavers all selling their wares. The quality varies, but overall it is extremely professional.

Vallauris has been a pottery town since Roman times, and today there are still over 200 potters working there, with at least a dozen showrooms lining the main street. Next door, the pretty village of Biot specialises in glass. Mougins, Vence and St-Paul-de-Vence are well known for their art galleries; Tourrettes-sur-Loup has a craft quarter in the old town, and the pedestrian streets of Menton are packed with craft and souvenir shops.

Confectionery. Local specialities include crystallised fruits and, from Tourrettes-sur-Loup (just outside Vence), crystal-lised violets. *Marrons glacés* (crystallised chestnuts) are the

⊘ PRODUCTS FROM THE OLIVE TREE

Introduced to southern France by the Greeks almost 3,000 years ago, olive trees are a feature of the regional landscape; their cultivation is an essential element in local culture. Buy olives loose from tubs in any market, or pre-packed in bottles or plastic containers. The favourite variety is the small black *olive de Nice*, but look as well for *pitchouline* (a green olive from the Var) and *tanche* (a purple olive from Nyons). Olives may be preserved in brine, but also come in oil seasoned with herbs, spices and hot peppers. Local olive oil is of high quality, notably that from around Grasse and Opio and in the Roya Valley – make sure it is labelled *huile d'olive vierge extra, première pression à froid*. Several artisanal oil mills have their own boutiques (pressing takes place from November to February, but most have shops open year-round). Another good buy are jars of *tapenade* (olive, caper and anchovy purée). There are also many items carved from the olive wood.

A mecca for all things pertaining to the olive tree is Alziari (www.alziari.fr), in the old town of Nice (next to the opera house), a wonderful shop where olives are stored in barrels and oil is poured from enormous vats.

speciality of Collobrières in the Maures.

Fabrics. Traditional Provençal cotton fabrics have gained considerable international popularity in recent years and are widely available on the coast. Market stalls carry stocks at very reasonable prices. Alternatively, two upmarket brands – Souleïado and Les Olivades – are much more expensive and sell from their own boutiques in all major towns.

Glassware in Biot

Fresh fruit and vegetables. Buy these from markets, or in season look for roadside stalls selling peaches, strawberries, melons and cherries.

Herbs. These grow wild on hillsides, but they are also extensively farmed for selling either fresh or dried. Look for *herbes de Provence* – a dried herb mixture often sold in pretty packages – and dried *bouquets garnis*, consisting of a bay leaf, rosemary and thyme. Alternatively, pick sprigs of sage, rosemary and thyme in the hills, and dry them at home.

Honey. Perfumed with lavender and herbs, honey is usually of excellent quality. Buy it from market stalls or from farms or producers who advertise at the roadside.

Perfumery. Grasse, the 'perfume capital', is the obvious place to go, but small shops also sell locally distilled lavender water, lavender bags, perfumed bath oils and soaps (soap-making is a traditional business of Marseille).

Santons. Look out for these quirky little figures in typical Provençal dress. They are on sale throughout the year, but are especially associated with Christmas – there are special *santon* fairs in December.

Wine. Provençal wines – red, rosé and white – are of excellent value. Among highly regarded French Riviera specialities

⊘ BEACHES

Although there are many superb expanses of natural sand, some beaches (notably at Monaco and Cannes) are created with imported sand. The beach at Nice is largely shingle. For fine golden sand, head for Juan-les-Pins and the Cap d'Antibes or the Var and the beaches in the Estérel, St-Tropez, Le Lavandou, the Cap de Brégancon and the Ile de Porquerolles.

Most beaches are free and can be very crowded in July and August. Private beaches attached to luxury hotels may be for residents only, though some may admit non-residents for a fee. Other private beaches are open to the fee-paying general public.

French Riviera beaches are not especially dangerous, nor are they affected by great tidal variations. Always take care, however, to swim within the designated swimming areas and to avoid the channels used by motorboats and jet skiers. Where there are strong currents or the seabed falls away steeply, this is clearly indicated. Petty theft is probably a greater hazard, so never leave personal belongings unattended. Jellyfish (*méduses*) are an increasing problem; look out for warning signs.

Topless bathing is accepted all along the French Riviera, but nudism is only tolerated on certain beaches. A few have been designated for the sole use of naturists, notably the Ile du Levant, an island off the Var coast (see page 80).

are wines from Bellet, a tiny and newly fashionable vineyard in the hills behind Nice, the Côtes de Provence, with especially good rosés, and Bandol. Buy the wines in a speciality shop or follow one of the *Routes du Vin* (wine roads). For a selection of everyday wines at low prices, stop at one of the *caves coopératives* (wine co-operatives) inland in the Var *département*.

Water sports in Cannes

SPORTS AND ACTIVITIES

Enjoy the outdoor life under the Mediterranean sun: facilities are generally first-rate and local tourist offices can usually provide information.

Boating and sailing. The coast is lined with yachting facilities, and boats of all sizes can be hired. Cannes and Antibes are the biggest rental centres. There are dinghy sailing schools at Bormes-les-Mimosas, Mandelieu-La Napoule and Menton.

Cycling. Hire a bike locally from a cycle shop, and pedal around the hills alongside the dedicated amateurs. The Estérel is especially good for cycling – Esterel Aventure (tel: 04 94 40 83 83) in St-Raphaël offers guided tours of the area on mountain bikes for four or more people. All tourist offices should have details and maps of local cycle routes.

Riding is a great way to explore inland

Fishing. You can spend a few hours with baited hook around the coast, or take a day-tour on a boat – try Alpha Marine (tel: 04 67 43 24 47) in Beaulieu-sur-Mer, Fréjus and Hyères; in the Var it's possible to accompany a local fisherman on his daily outing (known as Pescatourism). Many people like to angle for trout inland; enquire about licences at the local tourist office (see page 131) or town hall *(Hôtel de Ville* or *Mairie)*. See also www.peche-cote-azur.com.

Golf. French Riviera *parcours de golf* are among the best in France, with 18-hole courses at Mougins, Valbonne, Biot, Mandelieu-La Napoule (all clustered around Cannes), Monte Carlo (Mont-Agel), St-Raphaël, Ste-Maxime (Beauvallon) in the Var, and the two courses at the Terre Blanche Hotel at Tourrettes-sur-Loup. There are also a few nine-hole courses. See www.frenchriviera-tourism.com/golf for details.

Horse riding. There are lots of possibilities for riding, often 'ranch'-style in the countryside behind the coast. Explore the Mercantour National Park with Denis Longfellow (www.horse adventures.com, tel: 06 22 29 58 86) or the hills around Ste-Maxime with Ranch Eldorado (www.ranch-eldorado83.com, tel: 06 80 15 01 18).

Scuba diving and snorkelling. There's tremendous scope for divers. Instruction is available at centres in Nice, Monaco,

Cannes, St-Raphaël, Antibes, Bormes-les-Mimosas, Bandol and the Ile du Levant (off Hyères). The sea around the Iles d'Hyères contains over 500 shipwrecks. Diving from specially equipped boats is possible off the coast at Cavalaire and Le Lavandou.

Swimming. The French Riviera's beaches have a very good record for cleanliness. You will find many excellent sand beaches, as well as those with imported sand, rocks or pebbles (see page 88).

Water-skiing. *Le ski nautique* can be found at many larger beaches. For daredevils, wakeboarding is also available. Try Glisse Paradise (tel: 04 92 12 84 65) in St-Laurent-du-Var or Water Glisse Passion (tel: 06 61 85 59 27 or 06 61 13 32 40) in Ste-Maxime.

Windsurfing. *La planche à voile* is a well-established sport along the coast, with dozens of schools offering lessons or hiring out boards. Experienced surfers head for St-Laurent-du-Var, Six-Fours near Toulon and the Plage de l'Almanarre at Hyères.

Walking. The Riviera is great walking country. On the coast, the *sentier du littoral* or *sentier des douaniers* coast paths may be the only way to access the most beautiful parts of exclusive headlands, such as Cap d'Antibes, Cap Ferrat and Cap Martin, and often allow you to reach less crowded coves or to bathe from the rocks.

Walking in the hills of the Estérel, the Maures, Mont Faron or the backcountry behind Nice and Menton, even if only a few kilometres from the coast, can be a way to escape the throngs on the beach, with plenty to offer for serious walkers, notably in the Mercantour National Park.

In the Maures, guides from the Office National des Fôrets offer interesting accompanied walks taking in remote chapels, Neolithic dolmens or local wildlife. Details are available from tourist offices at Bormes-les-Mimosas and Collobrières.

Traversing the area are several Grandes Randonnées long-distance footpaths (indicated by red-and-white stripe markings), notably the GR 9, 51 and 90 in the Maures, GR 4 north of Grasse

Evening on the cours Saleya, Nice

and the GR 52, which crosses the Mercantour National Park. Details of these and other footpaths are published in *Topo Guides*; alternatively there are large-scale maps published by IGN. Note that many footpaths may be closed in high summer due to fire risk (check first at the local tourist office). Always take drinking water with you and never light fires.

Spectator sports. There are premier-division football teams at Nice and Monaco, and a rugby team at Toulon. Racecourses *(hippodromes)* are located at Cagnes-sur-Mer and at Hyères. Major sporting events in Monaco include the international men's tennis masters in April and the Monaco Grand Prix in May.

ENTERTAINMENT

The Riviera offers a huge choice of distractions to appeal to every taste. Nice, Toulon and Monte Carlo have **opera houses** staging concerts, ballet and opera, and in summer there are **jazz festivals** and **classical concerts** throughout the region. Jazz à Juan at Juan-les-Pins is the place to catch the big names of American jazz. Other top names play at Ramatuelle, while the Nice Jazz Festival also takes in rock, hip hop, world and electronic music. The classical Festival de Menton features singers and chamber-music ensembles.

Even the smallest village has a **patron saint's day** with processions, games and usually dancing. There are also numerous **traditional festivals** celebrating local produce, from sea urchins to lemons. La Fête de la Saint Pierre, patron saint of fishermen, is celebrated in many fishing ports, usually in late June or early July. Major events include Nice carnival during Mardi Gras (held February–March).

As for **nightlife**, sophisticated shows and elegant dinner-dancing venues are to be found at the international hotels in Nice, Cannes and Monte Carlo. Clubs flourish at all the coastal resorts, but those of St-Tropez, Monte Carlo and Cannes probably attract the most fashionable clientele.

If you're after glamour, head for the VIP Room (www.viproom.fr), Papagayo (www.papagayo-st-tropez.com) and Caves du Roy (www.lescavesduroy.com) in St-Tropez, Jimmy'z (www.jimmyz-montecarlo.com) and the Living Room in Monte Carlo, and Le Bâoli (www.lebaoli.com) and summer-only Le Palais (www.palais-cannes.com) at Cannes. La Siesta is a club on the beach at Antibes, open June and August, but its lounge bar, restaurant and casino are open all year. In Nice, Wayne's (www.waynes.fr) is one of several bars hosting live bands in the old town, and there are numerous stylish lounge bars with DJs at night.

Gambling has been part of the Riviera since the 19th

Open-air cinema

Cinema remains a passion in France. As well as multiplexes in the major towns, many resorts screen films in the open air during summer. The New Open Air Cinema (Terrasses du Parking-des-Pêcheurs) in Monaco shows films in VO (original language with French subtitles) every evening from July to early September on what it claims is the largest screen in Europe.

century. The Monte Carlo casino has the most cachet, but many resorts between Hyères and Menton have their own casinos. The smarter ones ask guests to be conservatively dressed; some charge an entrance fee (Monte Carlo is free). Operating hours vary, but general opening times are from 10am for slot machines and 8pm for gaming tables until 3am or 4am. The minimum age is 21, and you may be asked to show your passport.

CHILDREN

Children are very well catered for on the Riviera. Apart from some excellent beaches with water sports facilities, the mountain resorts of Valberg, Isola 2000 and Auron offer a range of summer activities, as well as skiing in winter. Many resorts put on extra summer entertainment, such as circuses.

There is a **zoo** on Mont Faron in Toulon (tel: 04 94 88 07 89) and a safari park at Fréjus (tel: 04 98 11 37 37).

Marineland (daily Apr–June, Sept 10am–7pm, July–Aug until 11pm, Oct–Dec and Feb–Mar until 6pm; www.marineland.fr) at Antibes is a winner with kids – a marine zoo with penguins, seals, sharks, and whale and dolphin shows. On the same site are **Aquasplash** (mid-June–Aug daily 10am–7pm), a water theme park with flumes, wave machines and pirate island, and the Jules Verne-themed **Adventure Golf** (daily July–Aug noon–midnight, times vary rest of year). Youngsters will adore **La Petite Ferme du Far West** (daily mid-June–Aug 10am–7pm, times vary rest of year), where there are baby farm animals, goats to milk and pony rides.

Attractions in Monaco include the **Musée Océanographique** (see page 47), an excellent aquarium; the **Jardin Animalier** (tel: +377 93 50 40 30), with its 250 exotic animals; and the **Jardin Exotique** (see page 47) with its collection of cacti.

CALENDAR OF EVENTS

January *Monaco*: circus festival. *Monte Carlo*: rally.

February *Bormes-les-Mimosas* (mid-month): Corso Fleuri parade of flower-decorated floats. *Menton* (second two weeks): lemon festival. *Nice* (two weeks preceding Shrove Tuesday): Mardi Gras carnival.

March Paris–Nice cycle race. *Tourrettes-sur-Loup:* violet festival.

April *Antibes*: Antiquités-Brocante du Vieil Antibes antiques fair. *Le Bar-sur-Loup* (Easter Mon): orange blossom festival. *Monte Carlo*: Printemps des Arts classical music and theatre festival; tennis championships.

May *Cannes*: international film festival. *Golfe-Juan*: re-enactment of Napoleon's landing in 1815. *Grasse*: rose festival. *Monte Carlo*: Monaco Grand Prix. *St-Tropez*: Bravade – costumed processions celebrating the town's patron saint, as well as the victory over the Spanish fleet in 1637.

Late May/early June *Antibes*: Voiles d'Antibes regatta for vintage yachts.

June *Fréjus*: sailing race. *St-Tropez* (15th): Bravade des Espagnols. Countrywide (21st): Fête de la Musique free concerts, mostly outdoors.

July Bastille Day (14th) with dancing and fireworks. *Antibes/Juan-les-Pins*: jazz festival. *Antibes*: Musiques au Coeur opera festival. *Cannes*: fireworks festival, dance music (Thursdays) on the beach. *Hyères*: Fête Médiévale and a Design Parade contemporary design festival (exhibitions until mid-Sept). *Nice/Cimiez*: jazz festival. *Ramatuelle*: jazz festival. *Vence*: Les Nuits du Sud world music festival (until early Aug).

August *Grasse*: festival of jasmine with floats, parades and dancing. *Menton*: classical music festival. *Monaco*: firework festival. *Ramatuelle* (mid-month): theatre festival.

September *Countrywide* (3rd weekend): Journées du Patrimoine heritage weekend. *Fréjus*: giant omelette festival. *Puget-Theniers* (first two weeks): patron saint's festival. *St-Tropez*: Voiles de St-Tropez yacht regatta.

October *Collobrières*: chestnut festival. *La Garde Freinet*: chestnut festival.

November *Cannes*: Festival de Danse (every other year, next 2019). *Monaco* (18th, 19th): Fête Nationale.

December *Bandol:* wine festival (first Sunday). *Nice*: outdoor Christmas market.

EATING OUT

Wining and dining is one of the delights of the French Riviera, whether it involves a simple snack at a pavement café, a romantic dinner served under the stars or one of the superb gastronomic meals created by a master chef. Alongside countless restaurants serving age-old regional favourites are places at which chefs put a creative spin on local cuisine.

The essence of southern French food is its emphasis on colour and full flavour, with fresh, basic ingredients such as tomatoes, garlic, onions, fresh herbs and olive oil. Fish is an important ingredient in coastal areas, and bread accompanies everything. The cuisine at the very eastern end of the Riviera is marked by its Italian past, with a variety of pasta dishes appearing on menus. Salads are firm favourites during the hot summer months, and fresh fruit – strawberries, raspberries, cherries, peaches, nectarines and melons – are plentiful.

WHEN TO EAT

Lunch is generally served from noon to 1.30 or 2pm. Holiday-makers, however, may prefer to have a snack or salad in a café or picnic lunch (you will find plenty of pre-cooked take-away goodies for a picnic at markets or from a butcher), with a main dinner at night. In the really smart resorts, restaurant service in the evening may continue until 10 or even 11pm, but do

Set menus

In addition to à la carte dishes off the main menu, most restaurants offer a choice of one or two set menus (menu formule or prix-fixe). These offer good value, especially at lunch-time, and may include wine.

not count on it in smaller towns, where last orders could be no later than 9pm.

WHAT TO EAT

Soup and salad

Pistou is a summer vegetable-and-pasta soup, taking its name from the *pistou* (a garlic-and-basil paste to which, around Nice, Parmesan may be added) that is stirred in at the last minute.

Lunching al fresco in Le Cannet

Soupe de poissons is made from small fish left over from the main catch, which are simmered with tomatoes and saffron, then puréed and sieved. It is always served with toasted bread, which should be rubbed with garlic cloves, spread with *rouille* (a pink, garlicky mayonnaise) and topped with grated cheese.

In a *bourride*, the fish is left in chunks and the sauce thickened with garlic mayonnaise.

Speaking of garlic, try a bracing *grand aïoli*, dipping boiled cod, potatoes, green beans and so on in the heavily garlic-flavoured mayonnaise. *Crudités* (chopped raw vegetables) might be served as an *anchoïade* or *bagna caouda* – to dip in a warm anchovy and olive oil sauce.

The *salade niçoise*, at its simple best, consists of tomatoes, anchovies and black olives moistened with olive oil and vinegar. Optional extras include raw vegetables such as sweet peppers, radishes, cucumber, young broad beans or artichokes,

Plate of scampi

onions, tuna and hard-boiled eggs. Lettuce and any cooked vegetables are anathema to purists.

Endless mixed salads are offered, many with seafood or ham and cheese. *Salade antiboise* usually combines cooked diced fish and anchovy fillets with green peppers, beetroot, rice and capers, dressed with vinaigrette.

Fish
Beach restaurants often serve excellent chargrilled fish. Sardines are the most common locally caught fish and may be served, very simply, dipped in hot oil and fried until crispy. To eat, hold by the tail and bite the fillet off either side, leaving the bones. They can also be filleted, opened flat, dipped in batter, fried in hot oil and served with a wedge of lemon *(beignets de sardine)*. Another local speciality – *sardines farcies* – is prepared by sandwiching two fillets together with a filling of chopped Swiss chard leaves, then frying or grilling the fish. Simplest of all is to marinate raw fillets in lemon juice until they turn opaque and are 'cooked' *(sardines marinées)*.

Loup de mer or *bar* (sea bass) is best prepared with fennel, flamed. Less expensive is *daurade* (sea bream), usually grilled or baked with onion, tomato, lemon juice and a dash of wine, occasionally with garlic and a *pastis* (aniseed) flavouring. *Rouget* (red mullet) may be served grilled or *en papillotte* (baked in foil with lemon wedges).

The scampi (langoustine or Dublin Bay prawns) that appear on menus everywhere can be good, but they're often imported and frozen. *Langouste*, or spiny lobster, costs a king's ransom. It's eaten cold with mayonnaise, or hot in a tomato-and-cognac sauce *(à l'américaine)*.

Mussels *(moules)* raised in the bay of Toulon are popular in white wine *(à la marinière)*, in soup or with savoury stuffings. A lowly but tempting gourmandise is *friture de mer* (whitebait), fried small fish that are eaten like French fries.

Meat and poultry

Steak turns up in various guises; the good cuts *(entrecôte, côte de bœuf, faux-filet, filet)* are just as tasty charcoal-grilled as they are with sauces. *Bleu* means almost raw; *saignant*, rare; *à point*, medium; and *bien cuit*, well done.

In springtime, lamb is particularly succulent; you will often see *gigot d'agneau* or *côtes d'agneau grillées aux herbes* (leg of lamb or grilled chops with herbs), which the French serve medium rare.

⊘ BOUILLABAISSE

The south's most famous fish soup is bouillabaisse. Although the Marseillais claim it as their own, it is found all along the Riviera coast. Several types of fish (in particular gurnard, scorpion fish and conger eel) are simmered with onion, leek, tomatoes and saffron, with mussels and potatoes added before the end. A complete meal rather than a soup, the broth is served first with croûtons and *rouille*, followed by the pieces of fish and potatoes. A good bouillabaisse is expensive and preferably ordered 24 hours in advance; some luxurious versions add lobster, but this is not really authentic.

The best lamb comes from the Alpes de Haute-Provence around Sisteron. *Brochettes*, or skewered kebabs, can be delicious.

Daube de bœuf, a traditional beef stew, is particularly good in Nice. With its aromatic, brown, wine-flavoured sauce, and accompanied by freshly made noodles *(pâtes fraîches)*, it can be truly memorable. *Estouffade*, a variation on the theme, adds black olives to the sauce. Left-over *daube* is the traditional filling of Nice-style ravioli.

Veal dishes are often of Italian inspiration, as in breaded *escalopes milanaises (scaloppini)*. *Alouettes sans têtes* are small rolled veal cutlets with stuffing.

Even tripe-haters may be converted by the Niçois version of this dish – *tripes niçoises* – a superb concoction simmered in olive oil, white wine, tomato, onion, garlic and herbs. *Pieds et paquets*, a speciality of Marseille, consists of stuffed tripe and sheeps' trotters simmered with bacon, onion, carrots, white wine, garlic and sometimes tomato.

Chicken is frequently spit-roasted with herbs *(poulet rôti aux herbes)*; *poulet niçois* is a fricassee made with white wine, stock, herbs, tomatoes and olives. Rabbit *(lapin)* might be served in a mustard sauce or *à la provençale*.

Winter warmers

In season (autumn/winter), the menu may list boar (marcassin or sanglier), venison (biche), partridge (perdreau), pigeon or quail (caille), often served with a grape sauce (aux raisins).

Pasta and vegetables

The Italian influence is strong around Menton and Nice, becoming less so as you travel further west, and pasta here rivals any you will find in Italy – but with subtle differences.

Ravioli and cannelloni are served with tomato sauce

Piles of fresh produce at Cannes' Marché Forville

or meat gravy, both topped with grated cheese – Parmesan, Gruyère or Emmental. Lasagne is popular, and fettucini, tagliatelle and spaghetti are frequently served as accompaniments to main meat dishes. Gnocchi (small, feather-light balls of semolina and/or mashed potato) are sprinkled with grated Gruyère and accompany meat dishes.

But the glory of southern France is its fresh vegetables. Ratatouille – a delicious stew of tomatoes, aubergine (eggplant), onions, courgette (zucchini) and green peppers – almost stands as a meal in itself. Other treats include marinated red peppers and courgette-flower fritters. You'll also find tomatoes baked with breadcrumbs, garlic and parsley *(tomates à la Provençale)* and vegetable *tians* (a type of gratin named after the oval earthenware dish), especially the *tian de courgettes* – a savoury egg, rice and courgette custard flavoured with garlic and herbs. A variety of baked summer vegetables stuffed with their own chopped insides, breadcrumbs or rice, and garlic, herbs, minced meat and grated cheese *(les petits farcis)* also feature on menus.

The stuffed vegetable speciality of the region is *chou fassum* (stuffed cabbage) from Grasse. At home, locals detach and blanch the outer leaves, then blanch and chop the inner leaves, mixing them with rice, eggs, cheese, herbs and minced meat. The cabbage is reassembled with the stuffing inside, tied up in a net bag (a *fassum*) and simmered for a couple of hours.

Asparagus *(asperges)* are superb served warm with melted butter or hollandaise sauce, or cold with vinaigrette. Artichokes receive the same treatment, or may appear with meat or herb stuffings; small local purple artichokes may be sliced thinly and eaten raw. In winter pumpkins, wild mushrooms and dishes with slivers of black truffle appear on many menus.

Lemon festival

For almost three weeks every February–March, Menton goes lemon crazy. Lemons and oranges are piled high into incredible sculptures in the Jardin des Bioves (themes have included carnivals, Disney characters and fairy tales), and on the Sundays floats and bands parade along the seafront, drawing thousands of tourists in homage to the fruit. See www.feteducitron.com.

Cheese and dessert

Don't miss out on the regionally made goat's or sheep's-milk cheeses *(fromages de chèvre/de brebis)*. A few good names to remember and try: *tomme de Sospel, tomme de chèvre de montagne, brousse de la Vésubie* and *poivre d'âne*.

For dessert, little can rival the local fruits in season. Savour the fat, dark-red strawberries (April–October) dipped in *crème fraîche*. Melons of all kinds (those from Cavaillon, near Aix, are renowned) taste sweeter than usual, and figs and peaches are equally good. Ice creams are good, especially the fruit sorbets. You can satisfy a sweet tooth with a variety of fruit tarts and local pastries: *ganses* (small fried cakes topped with sugar), *pignons* (buttery croissants with pine-nuts), lemon tart in Menton and the famed *tarte tropézienne* of St-Tropez – a sponge cake with custard filling and coarse-sugar topping.

Grapes and melons at the market on cours Saleya, Nice

Quick snacks

Cafés serve sandwiches on chunks of French bread, with pâté, ham or cheese being the most common fillings. Thin-sliced bread *(pain de mie)* is used for the delicious *croque-monsieur* (toasted ham and cheese sandwich). Omelettes are always reliable fare.

Be sure to sample *socca*, a speciality in the old town of Nice. A large wood-oven-baked pancake made from chickpea flour, it should be eaten piping hot, straight from the pan. *Tourte aux blettes* is a pie filled with swiss chard and raisins.

Another popular local item (perfect for the beach) is *pan bagnat* – essentially a huge round sandwich filled with tomatoes, hard-boiled egg, anchovies, olives, sliced raw onions and sometimes tuna, all moistened with a dash of olive oil.

Also noteworthy are the excellent thin-crusted pizzas, which come in numerous flavours and are always served with a bottle of fiery olive oil – spiced with hot peppers and herbs – for sprinkling over the top. *Pissaladière* is an open onion tart, flavoured with anchovies and topped with black olives.

Apéritifs and wine

Local Provençal wines tend to be light and are well suited to the climate and the cuisine. Rosés, always served well-chilled, are a speciality. They are served before a meal as an apéritif, but can also be sipped at any time of day. The whites are particularly good with seafood, and the reds (sometimes served very lightly chilled in summer) can stand up to any meat.

The best regional wines bear an *appellation d'origine contrôlée* (AOC) label. There are two AOC in the area covered in this guide, Côtes de Provence and Bellet, and a third, Bandol, beyond. Wine lists will also often feature wines from the nearby Coteaux d'Aix-en-Provence, Les Baux-de-Provence, Côtes de Luberon, Coteaux Varois and the southern Côtes du Rhône.

The largest Riviera appellation is Côtes de Provence, principally producing vast amounts of quaffable rosé wine, but also small quantities of white and some good-quality reds. The sole wine appellation in the Alpes-Maritimes *département* is Bellet on the edge of Nice, with just 60 hectares (150 acres) of vineyards under cultivation, producing white, red and rosé wines. Bandol, made in eight communes around the resort of Bandol west of Toulon, is the area's most prestigious appellation, notable for its excellent reds.

The favourite apéritif on the coast is undoubtedly *pastis* – a golden aniseed-flavoured liquid, which turns milky when water is added. With a dash of red grenadine liqueur, it becomes a *tomate*. Alternatively, try a *kir* (white wine with a dash of blackcurrant liqueur) or rosé wine with a dash of peach syrup.

TO HELP YOU ORDER ...

Do you have a table for...? **Avez-vous une table pour...?**

Do you have a fixed-price menu? **Avez-vous un menu à prix fixe?**

I'd like... **Je voudrais...**

beer la bière
bread le pain
butter le beurre
chips (fries) les frites
coffee le café
fish le poisson

meat la viande
menu la carte
milk le lait
soup le potage
water l'eau
wine le vin

... AND READ THE MENU

agneau lamb
ail garlic
anchois anchovy
asperges asparagus
aubergine aubergine/ eggplant
bar/loup de mer sea bass
bœuf beef
calmar squid
canard duck
champignon mushroom
chou cabbage
coquillages shellfish
crevettes prawns/shrimp
daurade sea bream
épinards spinach
flageolets bean sprouts
foie liver

fraises strawberries
framboises raspberries
fruits de mer seafood
gibier game
haricots verts green beans
jambon ham
langoustine scampi
lapin rabbit
moules mussels
pastèque watermelon
petits farcis stuffed vegetables
poivron bell pepper
pomme apple
pomme de terre potato
poulet chicken
veau veal

PLACES TO EAT

The price guidelines below are based on an average three-course meal for one person, excluding wine.

€€€€	over €90
€€€	€50–90
€€	€25–50
€	under €25

ANTIBES

The Golden Beef €€€ *Les Remparts, 1 avenue du Général Maizière, 06600 Antibes, tel: 04 93 34 59 86,* www.golden-beef.fr. The menu at this restaurant on the edge of old Antibes (north of waterfront garden) mainly consists of meat, however, pizza and salad are also available. There is a nice summer terrace to enjoy the warm climate. Open daily for lunch and dinner.

Les Vieux Murs €€€ *25 promenade Amiral de Grasse, 06600 Antibes, tel: 04 93 34 06 73,* www.lesvieuxmurs.com. Highly regarded restaurant located in vaulted rooms in the port's old ramparts on the waterfront south of the Musée Picasso. Open daily for lunch and dinner.

BIOT

Les Arcades €€ *16 place des Arcades, 06410 Biot, tel: 04 93 65 01 04,* www.hotel-restaurant-les-arcades.com. Something of an institution, this popular 15th-century village inn that doubles as an art gallery serves Provençal cuisine in a small dining room, or outside under medieval arcades. Also has twelve characterful bedrooms with antique furnishings (**€€**). Closed Sun dinner, Mon and mid-Nov–mid-Dec.

BORMES-LES-MIMOSAS

La Tonnelle €€ *place Gambetta, 83230 Bormes-les-Mimosas, tel: 04 94 71 34 84,* www.restaurant-la-tonnelle.com. Situated in a pleasant, airy dining room in Bormes village. Attractively presented modern Mediterranean cooking by owner-chef Gil Renard includes such dishes as tuna tartare with artichokes or land-sea combinations like lamb with anchovies, home-made bread and inventive desserts. Open for lunch and dinner Wed-Sun.

CAGNES-SUR-MER

Fleur de Sel €€€ *85 montée de la Bourgade, 06800 Haut-de-Cagnes, tel: 04 93 20 33 33*, www.restaurant-fleurdesel.com. Gourmet seasonal cui-sine with a southern accent is served in the rustic dining room of an old house in the heart of this charming village. Try beef fillet with truffles followed by caramelised Menton lemon accompanied by mandarin sor-bet. Dinner only. Closed Wed all year round and Thu Oct–Mar.

CANNES

Aux Bons Enfants € *80 rue Meynadier, 06400 Cannes,* www.aux-bons-enfants-cannes.com. Located in a backstreet behind the port, this is a simple family-run bistro serving excellent home cooking. Closed Sun, Mon and throughout Dec. No credit cards.

Caffé Roma €€ *1 square Mérimée, 06400 Cannes, tel: 04 93 38 05 04*, www.cafferoma.fr. A chic and lively rendezvous opposite the Palais, with a terrace. Serves cocktails alongside an Italian menu, with a relatively good value *plat du jour* (dish of the day) and excellent ice creams. Serves until 1am.

Chez Vincent et Nicolas €€ *90 rue Meynadier, 06400 Cannes, tel: 04 93 68 35 39*, www.chezvincentetnicolas.fr. Trendy address with lively atmos-phere, exposed stone walls, candlelit tables and cooking TV broadcast while you eat. Updated bistro favourites served until midnight. Closed Mon in low season. Open only for dinner.

La Palme d'Or €€€€ *Hôtel Martinez, 73 boulevard de la Croisette, 06400 Cannes, tel: 04 92 98 74 14*, www.hotel-martinez.com. One of the best gourmet addresses on the Riviera where the dinner for Cannes Film Festival's Palme d'Or jury is held each year. Closed Sun. The hotel also has a beach restaurant, ZPlage (**€€€**), which is equally as glamorous.

GRIMAUD

Le Coteau Fleuri €€€ *place des Pénitants, 83310 Grimaud, tel: 04 94 43 20 17.* Popular 18th-century hotel/restaurant quietly situated in the old village. Renowned locally for Jean-Claud Paillard's gastronomic take on regional cuisine. Has a terrace, Provençal décor and a welcoming atmosphere, plus 14 bedrooms (**€€**). Closed Tue Sept–June.

HYÈRES

La Colombe €€€ *663 route de Toulon, quartier de la Bayorre, 83400 Hyères, tel: 04 94 35 35 16,* www.restaurantlacolombe.com. An attractive restaurant with excellent cooking by owner-chef Pascal Bonomy. Serves seafood, Provence-inspired dishes and interesting local wines. Closed Mon, Tue lunch and Sat lunch July–Aug, Mon, Sat lunch and Sun eve Sept–June.

LE LAVANDOU

Les Tamaris 'Chez Raymond' €€ *plage de Saint Clair, 83980 Le Lavandou, tel: 04 94 71 07 22.* Right on the waterfront, this family-run restaurant has been serving seafood to locals and visitors for 50 years. Try lobster with spaghetti followed by their award-winning ice-cream washed down with a Varois wine. Closed Tue and Dec–Feb.

MENTON

A Braijade Meridounale € *66 rue Longue (parallel to quai Bonaparte), 06500 Menton, tel: 04 93 35 65 65,* www.abraijade.fr. Authentic regional cooking is served in an ancient beamed dining room up in the old town. Specialities include vegetable fritters, grilled skewered meats and fish, ravioli with pistou sauce (the local version of pesto) and the *bagna caouda* (or *anchoïade*). Open for lunch Mon–Fri, daily for dinner.

MONACO

Café de Paris €€ *place du Casino, 98000 Monaco, tel: 377-98 06 76 23,* www.casinocafedeparis.com. A faithful recreation of the original *belle* *époque* bar and brasserie, next to the casino, plus a restaurant with 1900s décor and slot machines. Great people-watching from the pavement terrace. The *crêpe suzette* was invented here. Serves all day.

Le Louis XV €€€€ *Hôtel de Paris, place du Casino, 98000 Monaco, tel: 377-98 06 88 64, www.ducasse-paris.com.* One of the most glamorous restaurants in Europe, with sumptuous décor and immaculate service. The acclaimed cuisine by Alain Ducasse's protégé Franck Cerrutti takes Mediterranean cooking to the heights of haute cuisine. Advance booking necessary. Open for lunch Fri–Mon, dinner Thu–Mon except July–Aug when it is also open Wed evenings. Closed end Nov–end Dec.

SenSais €€€ *2 Rue du Portier, 98000 Monaco, tel: 377-93 30 30 70, www.sensais.mc.* The cosmopolitan, Italian décor reflects the menu which is inspired by Italian and French classics. The Royal Bouillabaisse, the traditional southern dish, is especially good here. A special lunch menu is available as well as a set three-course dinner menu. Open daily for lunch and dinner.

MOUGINS

Le Bistrot de Mougins €€€ *place du Village, 06250 Mougins, tel: 04 93 75 78 34.* In the centre of Mougins, in the vaulted cellars of an old coaching inn, you'll find traditional Provence-inspired cooking. Popular and reasonably priced (by Mougins standards) so booking is advised. Closed Wed and mid-Nov–mid-Dec.

Le Candille €€€€ *Le Mas Candille, boulevard Clément Rebuffel, 06250 Mougins, tel: 04 92 28 43 43, www.lemascandille.com.* One of the loveliest restaurants in one of the loveliest hotels on the French Riviera. Enjoy the views over the countryside while savouring Serge Gouloumes' mouthwatering creations such as crab soufflé with caviar or breast of pigeon with soy caramel glaze. Open for dinner Tue–Sat.

NICE

L'Ane Rouge €€€ *7 quai des Deux Emmanuel, 06000 Nice, tel: 04 93 89 49 63, www.anerougenice.com.* This is the best of the fish restaurants on the old port. It has an excellent selection of white wines, and a terrace to enjoy them on. Closed Wed, lunch Thu and two weeks in February.

Le Bistrot Gourmand €€€ *3 rue Desboutin, 06000 Nice, tel: 04 92 14 55 55.* Opened in 2010, this stylish gourmet restaurant in the far west of the old town has good value set menus with a lunchtime two-course menu for less than €20. House specialities include bouillabaisse, risotto and soufflé. Closed Sun.

L'Escalinada €€ *22 rue Pairolière, 06000 Nice, tel: 04 93 62 11 71,* www.escalinada.fr. Genuine Niçoise cuisine in the north of old Nice. Specialities include ravioli and gnocchi plus the traditional *socca*. Closed for dinner Sunday.

La Merenda €€ *4 rue Raoul Bosio, 06000 Nice.* Authentic Niçois bistro in the heart of old Nice behind the law courts. Orders taken until 9.30pm. Closed 1–15 Aug and Sat–Sun. No credit cards.

Le Safari €€ *1 cours Saleya, 06000 Nice, tel: 04 93 80 18 44,* www.restaurantsafari.fr. This market-side brasserie is a Niçois institution, with high-speed waiters and a good people-watching terrace. Well-prepared local specialities as well as pizza and fish are served.

ST-JEAN-CAP-FERRAT

Paloma Beach €€€ *1 route de Sainte-Hospice, 06230 St-Jean-Cap-Ferrat, tel: 04 93 01 64 71,* www.paloma-beach.com. The main reason to come here is the location: on the beach in one of the most glamorous parts of the world. Watch the yachts bobbing in the bay as you tuck into fish or salad niçoise. You might even find yourself sitting near Sir Mick Jagger or Tom Cruise. Valet parking. Closed Oct–Easter.

ST-RAPHAËL

Elly's €€€ *54 rue de la Liberté (east of the town hall), 83700 St-Raphaël, tel: 04 94 83 63 39,* www.elly-s.com. Traditional French produce is given a contemporary twist by chef Franck Chabod and the presentation of the dishes is as beautiful as the artworks on the walls. Has an interior courtyard. Closed Sun–Mon.

ST-TROPEZ

Le Girelier €€€ *Le Port des Pêcheurs, quai Jean Jaurès, 83990 St-Tropez,* *tel: 04 94 97 03 87,* www.legirelier.fr. This ever-fashionable quayside fish restaurant has a chic fisherman's-shack-inspired décor designed by Kristian Gavoille. Fish *a la plancha* is a speciality. Service all day, with outdoor dining during the summer. Closed Nov–Mar.

Spoon Byblos €€€ *avenue Paul Signac (opposite Citadelle), 83990 St-Tropez, tel: 04 94 56 68 19,* www.byblos.com. Alain Ducasse's mix-and-match world food concept allows you to put together different sauces and accompaniments with your lacquered beef, seared tuna or scallop kebab, with a Mediterranean emphasis. It's within the Byblos Hotel. Open Easter–mid-Oct, dinner only.

TOULON

La Promesse €€ *250 rue Jean Jaurès (south of opera house), 83000 Toulon, tel: 04 94 98 79 39,* www.restaurant-lapromesse.fr. Owner-chef Valérie Costa's dishes are inspired by the cooking of her Italian grandmothers and her travels around the world. The menu changes daily and there is a good selection of wines. Closed Sun, Mon and mid-July–mid-Aug.

LA TURBIE

Le Café de la Fontaine €€ *4 avenue du Général de Gaulle, 06320 La Turbie, tel: 04 93 28 52 79,* www.hostelleriejerome.com. Chef Bruno Cirino of the acclaimed Hostellerie Jérôme serves fresh regional specialities at re-markable prices in this relaxed gourmet bistro. Booking recommended. Closed Mon in winter. Visa and Mastercard only.

VENCE

La Litote €–€€ *5–7 rue de l'Evêché, 06140 Vence, tel: 04 93 24 27 82.* Lamb with pesto and tuna with organic quinoa can feature on the regularly chang-ing menu of this old town restaurant whose terrace is in a charming square. Closed Sun, Mon and Tue. The adjoining shop sells good quality local produce.

A–Z TRAVEL TIPS

A SUMMARY OF PRACTICAL INFORMATION

A

ACCOMMODATION (See also Camping, Youth hostels and the list of Recommended hotels starting on page 134)

While the French Riviera has more than its fair share of luxury hotels, it is possible to find a wide range of very acceptable accommodation to fit all budgets. Official classification is from one to five stars (some hotels are outside this classification, but this does not imply that they are inferior). Star ratings are based on facilities, customer service, accessibility and sustainable development. Even many two-star hotels now have air-conditioning. Excellent hotels can be found in all categories. Be warned that the best establishments within each price range are extremely popular, and advance booking is advised.

Apart from hotels in the one-star range, most rooms have a private bath or shower/WC, telephone and TV. Three-star rooms will have additional facilities such as a hairdryer and minibar. Swimming pools are common, but not all hotels have a restaurant, although breakfast is usually provided, at extra charge. Only luxury hotels have room service and an in-house laundry, and may also offer all sorts of services from DVD players to boat and helicopter hire. Spas and fitness rooms are increasingly popular. Hotel reception staff can often speak English.

Peak season. July and August are peak months, when prices are highest and rooms at a premium. During May – when both the Cannes Film Festival and Monaco Grand Prix are staged – every room from St-Tropez to the Italian border is booked months, sometimes years, in advance. If you intend to be here at that time, plan well ahead.

Low season. The larger centres such as Nice, Cannes and Monte Carlo have a calendar of international conferences to attract visitors throughout the winter. Many hotels, however, particularly inland and in smaller seaside resorts, close during these months. Those that do remain open frequently offer substantial reductions in room rates; look out for special offers on the internet.

If booking ahead, the hotel may ask for a **deposit**, or *arrhes*, but is now more likely to request your credit card number. For last-minute bookings without a deposit, the reservation will usually be honoured until 6pm, but may be given to another client if you have not arrived, or telephoned to explain, before that time.

If looking for last-minute accommodation, tourist offices often have lists of hotels where rooms are still available or may be able to find a room for you; larger offices may have a direct booking service.

Types of hotel and rented accommodation include:

Relais et Châteaux (www.relaischateaux.com). These luxury hotels are four and five-star establishments, some in historical buildings, and many have gastronomic restaurants.

Châteaux et Hôtels Collection (www.chateauxhotels.com). An upmarket group of independently owned hotels, ranging from luxurious châteaux to charming rural hotels and classic city hotels, many with good restaurants.

Relais du Silence (www.silencehotel.com). A chain of two- to four-star hotels in particularly calm and scenic settings.

Logis de France (www.logishotels.com). Small or medium-sized, family-run restaurant/hotels, mostly in the two-star bracket, almost all of which lie in villages or the countryside. The *Logis de France* publishes an annual guide (free if requested from the French national tourist offices abroad). Although each establishment can be very different, their charter requires a personalised welcome and regional cooking using local produce.

> Do you have a single/double room for tonight? **Avez-vous une chambre pour une/deux personne(s) pour ce soir?**
> with bath/shower/toilet **avec bain/douche/toilettes**
> What's the rate per night? **Quel est le prix pour une nuit?**

Hotel chains. The **Accor** group (www.accorhotels.com) encompasses several chains covering all budgets, from the upmarket Pullmann and

Mercure hotels, modern Novotel and All Seasons, mid-range Ibis to budget Etap Hôtel and economy Formule 1. Most are located in urban areas. Another group is **Louvre Hotels** (www.louvrehotels.com), with the upmarket Golden Tulip, mid-range Kyriad, budget Campanile and economy Première Classe chains.

Aparthotels. These are halfway between hotel and apartment, with a kitchenette and a generally lower degree of service than in a hotel. Usually studio or two-room accommodation. Two main chains are Citadines (www.citadines.com) and Suite Novotel (www.novotel.accorhotels.com).

Chambres d'hôtes. This is bed and breakfast in the homes of private individuals, and varies from very simple budget accommodation to upmarket rooms in period properties with beautiful decoration and correspondingly high prices. A generous breakfast is always included in the price; there may also be a *table d'hôte* (dinner) for an extra sum. With a maximum of six rooms, and the chance to talk to your hosts, this can be a convivial experience of the real France. Some *chambres d'hôtes* are classified by the Gîtes de France group, while others are registered with their local tourist office.

Gîtes ruraux. The Gîtes de France, an official body with regional offices, oversees the organisation of self-catering holiday accommodation and sets standards. Accommodation is usually in lovely old regional houses or renovated farm buildings. Certain minimal standards of comfort are required. Each *gîte* is rented by the week (changeover on Saturday) or sometimes for weekends in low season. You can consult and reserve *gîtes* on www.gites-de-france.com or book directly with the owners.

Villas and seaside flats. Numerous agencies rent privately owned villas and holiday flats in and around the coastal resorts. Try Côte d'Azur Collection (www.cotedazurcollection.co.uk), Air BnB (www.airbnb.com) and Chez Nous (www.cheznous.com).

AIRPORTS *(aéroports)*

Nice-Côte d'Azur is the main international airport (tel: 08 20 42 33 33; www.nice.aeroport.fr), with scheduled connections from all major European cities, North Africa and some American cities.

There are also international airports at **Toulon (Hyères)** (www.toulon-hyeres.aeroport.fr) and **Marseille** (www.marseilleairport.com).

From the UK there are many low-cost flights to the region:

Aer Lingus (Ireland tel: 0818 365 000, France tel: 08 21 23 02 67; www.aerlingus.com) flies from Dublin and Cork to Nice and from Dublin to Marseille.

Air France (UK tel: 0207 660 0337, France tel: 08 92 70 26 54; www.airfrance.com) flies from London Heathrow or City via Paris to Nice, Marseille and Toulon.

British Airways (UK tel: 0844 493 0787, France tel: 08 25 82 54 00; www.britishairways.com) operates flights from London Heathrow and Gatwick to Nice and Marseille.

easyJet (UK tel: 0843 104 5000, France tel: 08 20 42 03 15; www.easyjet.com) flies to Nice from Belfast, Bristol, Edinburgh, Gatwick, Liverpool, Luton, Newcastle and Stansted, and Marseille from Bristol and Gatwick.

Flybe (UK tel: 0871 700 2000, France tel: 01 39 22 68 529; www.flybe.com) flies from Southampton to Nice and Toulon.

Jet2 (UK tel: 0871 226 1737, France tel: 08 21 23 02 03; www.jet2.com) flies from Glasgow, Leeds, Manchester and East Midlands to Nice.

Ryanair (UK tel: 0871 246 0000, France tel: 08 92 56 21 50; www.ryanair.com) flies from Dublin to Nice.

Buses depart from Nice airport for all main destinations along the coast, and a shuttle takes passengers into Nice, stopping at major hotels and the mainline station. Some hotels run their own free minibus service. Taxis are also readily available.

B

BUDGETING FOR YOUR TRIP

The following are some approximate prices in euros (€):

Bicycle and moped hire. Bicycle €20–30 per day, depending on type of bike, deposit €150–450; moped €40–70, deposit €450–750.

Camping. €30–50 per night for four persons with tent or caravan.

Car hire. €32–120 a day for an economy model. There are often deals if you book at the same time as a flight or train.

Entertainment. Cinema €10. Nightclub/casino admission often 'free' but with a premium on drinks. Opera ticket €15–80.

Meals and drinks. Breakfast €10–25 depending on category of hotel. In restaurants in the evening expect to pay from around €25 for three courses, not including wine, in a budget establishment, €35–45 in a good bistro, €35–60 in a trendy beachside establishment, and €100 or more in a top gastronomic restaurant. Many restaurants offer good-value menus at lunchtime. Coffee €2.90–3.50; whisky or cocktail €4–8; 25cl beer €5–6; sandwich in a café €9.50; salad in a café €10–15.

Museums. Free–€10.

Sports. Windsurf board hire about €15 an hour, €200 a week, instruction (with board, one lesson per day over one week) €90–120, water-skiing (10 minutes) €20, tennis €15 an hour for a court, golf €25–50 (9-hole), €65–180 (18-hole).

C

CAMPING *(le camping)*

Campers (with caravans and tents) are well catered for, with a choice of two- to four-star sites. Many sites also have permanent chalets to rent. Most have showers, a swimming pool, children's play areas, tent and bike rental, and bar/restaurant. Some are adjacent to beaches and others attached to farms. Early booking for July/August is advisable. See also www.campingfrance.com.

Camping outside recognised sites *(camping sauvage)* is illegal.

CAR HIRE *(location de voitures; see also Driving)*

Local car-hire firms sometimes offer lower prices than the international companies, but may not let you return the car elsewhere, at a convenient drop-off point.

To hire a car, you must have a driving licence (held for at least one year) and a passport. The minimum age varies from 20 to 23. A substantial deposit (refundable) is usually required, unless you hold a recognised credit card. You will be asked for proof of your local or hotel address. Third-party insurance is compulsory. Major car-hire companies include:

Avis: tel: 08 21 23 07 60; 08 206 11 32, www.avis.com
Budget: tel: 08 25 00 35 64; 08 21 230 386, www.budget.com
Europcar: tel: 08 25 35 83 58; 08 258 100 81, www.europcar.com
Hertz: tel: 08 25 86 18 61; 08 25 342 343, www.hertz-europe.com
Rent-a-Car: tel: 08 91 70 02 00, www.rentacar.fr

> I'd like to rent a car today/tomorrow **Je voudrais louer une voiture aujourd'hui/demain**
> for one day/a week **pour un jour/une semaine**

CLIMATE

The French Riviera enjoys a typical Mediterranean climate; that is to say, hot, dry summers, mild and wet weather in spring and autumn, and short winters that are usually quite mild but with cold spells. The area is also occasionally affected by the mistral – a strong, cold wind that blows down the Rhône Valley and along the coast. There are often thunderstorms at night in late August. Below are some average monthly temperatures, though peak temperatures can be much higher:

	J	F	M	A	M	J	J	A	S	O	N	D
Air °C	9	9	11	13	17	20	23	22	20	17	12	9
Air °F	48	48	52	55	63	68	73	72	68	63	54	48
Sea °C	13	13	13	15	17	21	24	25	23	20	17	14
Sea °F	55	55	55	59	63	70	75	77	73	68	63	57

CLOTHING

The Riviera resorts are probably the most dressed-up part of France, although only the most formal of restaurants or casinos will require gentlemen to wear a jacket and tie *(tenue correcte)*. Smart, casual attire is the norm. Jeans are universally acceptable.

Even in summer, a jumper or wrap is useful for cooler evenings, and a waterproof coat or jacket will be needed from October to April. Comfortable shoes are advisable for sightseeing.

CRIME AND SAFETY (See also Emergencies and Police)

Inevitably a prosperous area such as the French Riviera attracts petty criminals, and the major cities have some security problems, but incidents of violent crime against visitors are rare. Normal precautions apply. Try not to carry large amounts of cash, never leave valuables in your car, and be alert for pickpockets, especially in crowds. Any loss or theft should be reported immediately to the nearest *commissariat de police* or *gendarmerie*. Demonstrations occur regularly in major cities around France; it is best to avoid these.

Due to the increased threat of terrorism in France access to public areas may be restricted at times and there may be additional security officers patrolling the streets. Borders checks may be more stringent.

D

DISABLED TRAVELLERS

Airports, hotels, museums and other establishments are gradually equipping themselves to assist travellers with disabilities. A tour operator can help you to tailor your holiday, and regional tourist offices will also be able to provide information (see page 131). The Association des Paralysés de France (13 place de Rungis, 75013 Paris, tel: 01 53 80 92 97, www.apf.asso.fr) publishes a *Guide Vacances* which lists accommodation suitable for disabled travellers.

DRIVING (See also Car hire)

To take a car into France you'll need a valid driving licence, your car registration papers, insurance coverage (the green card is no longer obligatory for members of EU countries, but comprehensive coverage is strongly advisable), a red warning triangle, a reflective jacket, a breathalyser and a set of spare bulbs.

Drivers and all passengers (back and front) are required by law to wear seatbelts (where fitted in the back). Children under the age of 10 may not travel in the front of the car. Driving on a foreign provisional licence is not permitted, and the minimum driving age is 18.

Driving regulations. Drive on the right, pass on the left. In built-up areas, give priority to vehicles coming from the right. At a roundabout (*giratoire/rond-point*), drivers already on the roundabout always have priority over those entering it, indicated by markings on the road.

Speed limits. When conditions are dry, the limit is 130km/h (80mph) on motorways (expressways), 110km/h (70mph) on dual carriageways, 90km/h (55mph) on other country roads, 50km/h (30mph) in built-up areas and 30km/h (18mph) in some residential districts. Speed limits are reduced in wet weather.

Signposting is generally good. Tourist sights are usually highlighted with a brown symbol, making it easy to distinguish them. A blue road sign directs you to an *autoroute* (motorway), a green one to a *route nationale* (RN: main road) and white to secondary 'D' roads. 'C' roads are

accotements non stabilises soft shoulders
chaussée déformée uneven road surface
deviation diversion (detour)
péage toll
priorité à droite give way to traffic from right
ralentir slow down
serrez à droite/à gauche keep right/left

tiny communal roads. For ramblers, red-and-white markings indicate that the path is on a 'GR' *(grande randonnée)* trail.

Road conditions. Provence and the Riviera are well served with motorways, particularly if you are coming from Paris (the north–south axis), though roads can get clogged up in summer with huge traffic jams on Saturdays and around the 14 July and 15 August public holidays. The roads are often less busy at lunchtime, and also on Sunday, when commercial trucks are not allowed to travel.

Parking *(stationnement).* This is sometimes impossible in the height of summer, and often difficult the rest of the year. If possible, park outside the town centre and go by foot. Most major tourist sights have parking areas. Individual meters have now largely been replaced by pay-and-display ticket machines, taking either coins or special cards. Parking discs for 'zones bleus' can be obtained from police stations or tourist offices.

Touristy villages such as St-Paul-de-Vence and Haut-de-Cagnes may insist you leave your car outside the old centre. Major towns, such as Nice, Cannes and Toulon, have several underground car parks. *Stationnement interdit* means 'no parking'. *Sauf riverains* means 'except residents'. Don't leave your car in a *zone piétonne* (pedestrian precinct), or where the sign says *stationnement gênant* (parking obstructive). A pictograph shows your car's fate...being towed away.

Breakdowns *(panne).* There are emergency phones every 20km (12 miles) on main roads, connected to local police stations that function around the clock. Elsewhere, dial 17, wherever you are, and the police will put you in touch with a garage that will come to your rescue – at a price, of course, so it's wise to take out international breakdown insurance before leaving home. Local garages usually provide towing facilities and spare parts for European cars. Ask for an estimate before authorising repairs and expect to pay value-added tax (TVA) on top.

Fuel and oil *(essence; huile).* Unleaded petrol *(essence sans plomb)* and diesel *(gasoil)* are the norm in France. Most fuel stations are self-service. It's worth filling up on Saturday, since many garages close on Sunday, although large supermarkets often have 24-hour petrol pumps for use with credit cards. Fuel tends to be more expensive on motorways, so go to supermarkets instead. A map showing filling stations can be obtained from tourist offices.

Motorcycles. As of 2013 all motorcyclists and their passengers must wear reflective clothing on the upper part of their body.

---

driving licence **permis de conduire**
car registration papers **carte grise**
Are we on the right road for...? **Sommes-nous sur la route de...?**
Fill the tank, please. **Le plein, s'il vous plaît.**
I've broken down. **Ma voiture est en panne.**
There's been an accident. **Il y a eu un accident.**

E

ELECTRICITY

220-volt, 50-cycle AC is universal. British visitors should remember to buy an adaptor *(adaptateur)*; American visitors will need a transformer *(transformateur)*.

EMBASSIES AND CONSULATES

Most consulates are open from Monday to Friday, from 9 or 10am to 4 or 5pm with an hour or so off for lunch.

Australia: (Embassy) 4 rue Jean-Rey, 75015 Paris, tel: 01 40 59 33 00, www.france.embassy.gov.au

Canada: (Consulate) 35 avenue Montaigne, 75008 Paris, tel: 01 44 43 29 02, www.embassy-canada.com

Ireland: (Embassy) 12 avenue Foch, 75116 Paris, tel: 01 44 17 67 00, www.ie/irish-embassy/france

UK: (Consulate) 10 Place de la Joliette, Marseille 13006, tel: 04 91 15 72

10, www.gov.uk/world/france
US: (Consulate General) 12 place Valerian Fry, 13086 Marseille, tel: 01 43 12 48 85, http://fr.usembassy.gov/consulara

EMERGENCIES *(urgences; see also Police)*

In case of an emergency, dial **17** for the police *(police-secours)* and **18** for the fire brigade *(sapeurs-pompiers)*, who will also answer medical emergencies. Dial **15** for an ambulance. Dial **112** from a mobile phone.

G

GETTING THERE (see also Airports)

By car. The 1,200km (750-mile) *autoroute* trip from Calais to Nice (via Reims and bypassing Paris) can take as little as 15 hours, or you can stay overnight at one of the *autoroute* hotels. However, *péage* (toll) fees are expensive, and drivers who prefer a cheaper, more leisurely trip often opt to use both *autoroutes* and other roads. For toll estimates and route-planning, see www.mappy.fr or www.viamichelin.fr.

By bus. The cheapest way to get to the Riviera is by bus. Flixbus (tel: (855) 626 8585; www.flixbus.com) has services from London to Cannes, Aix-en-Provence, Toulon and Nice.

By train. From the UK, Eurostar trains (tel: 08432 186 186; www.eurostar. co.uk) run from London, Ebbsfleet and Ashford to Paris Gare du Nord. Services for the South depart from the Gare de Lyon. The high-speed TGV reaches Marseille in about 3 hours, Nice in 6 hours. In the UK, tickets can be booked at the Rail Europe Travel Centre (193 Piccadilly, London W1J 9EU; tel: 0844 848 4078) or online at www.raileurope.co.uk. For SNCF reservations and information, visit www.voyages-sncf.com. US visitors can call 1-800 622 8600 or visit www.raileurope.com/us. Ask about passes and discounts.

By motor-rail. The SNCF operates a year-round AutoTrain service from Paris to Marseille, Toulon, St-Raphaël and Nice; you make your own way to your chosen destination and pick up your car at the station (tel: 08448 484 050; www.raileurope.co.uk).

H

HEALTH AND MEDICAL CARE (See also Emergencies)

EU nationals staying in France are entitled to use the French Social Security system, which refunds up to 70 percent of medical expenses. To get a refund, British nationals should obtain a European Health Insurance Card before leaving the UK. These are available online at www.ehic.org.uk or from post offices.

If you have treatment while in France, the doctor will give you a prescription and a *feuille de soins* (statement of treatment). The medication will carry *vignettes* (stickers), which you stick onto your *feuille de soins*. Send this, the prescription and your European Health Insurance Card to the local Caisse Primaire d'Assurance Maladie (in the phone book under Sécurité Sociale). Refunds can take over a month.

Nationals of non-EU countries should take out travel and medical insurance before leaving home. Medical consultations and prescriptions have to be paid for in full at the time of treatment.

If you are ill, your hotel can probably recommend an English-speaking doctor or dentist; otherwise, ask at the tourist office or, in an emergency, the *gendarmerie*. Chemists *(pharmacies)* display green crosses. Staff are helpful in dealing with minor ailments and can recommend a nurse *(infirmière)* if you need other care. The name and address of the local night-duty chemist is displayed in the window of other pharmacies – the *gendarmerie* or local papers will also have it.

L

LANGUAGE

Southern French has a warm, charming accent, drawing out syllables in a way you don't hear elsewhere in the country and placing extra emphasis on the end of words or sentences. The usual nasal French 'en' ending becomes a hard 'ng' (*chien* sounds like *chieng*).

In addition, you'll hear all sorts of rolling, vaguely Italianate dialects, especially Niçois and Monégasque.

good morning/good afternoon **bonjour**
good afternoon/good evening **bonsoir**
goodbye **au revoir**
Is there anyone here who speaks English? **Y a-t-il quelqu'un ici qui parle anglais?**
yes/no **oui/non**
please/thank you **s'il vous plaît/merci**
excuse me **excusez-moi**
where?/when?/how? **où?/quand?/comment?**
how much? **combien?**

LGBTQ TRAVELLERS

The Riviera is generally a gay-tolerant area, especially in the big cities, notably Nice where there are several gay venues and a lively annual Pink Pride parade in June. *Nice Practical Guide*, published by the tourist office, lists gay bars and clubs. Coco Beach in Nice and the naturist beach of Ile du Levant are particularly popular with the gay crowd.

M

MEDIA

Newspapers and magazines *(journaux/revues)*. *Nice Matin* and *La Provence* are the two leading local dailies, but the main French nationals are also available and newsagents in most coastal towns carry a selection of British newspapers and magazines. The Paris-based *International Herald Tribune* is widely available, as is *USA Today*. Look out for the *Riviera Reporter* (www.rivierareporter.com) and the *Riviera*

Times (www.rivieratimes.com), which give an irreverent, insider's view of the region.

Television and radio. France has five main TV channels, plus the subscription channel Canal+ and numerous cable and satellite channels, often including BBC World or CNN. National radio stations include France Inter (FM 87.8 MHz) and France Info (FM 105.5 MHz). RFI (Radio France International) has English-language bulletins and BBC World Service is available at certain times of day on short-wave radio. On motorways, Autoroute FM (107.7 MHz) has bulletins in English in summer. Monte Carlo's Riviera Radio (106.3 and 106.5 MHz) is an all-English station.

MONEY

Currency *(monnaie)*. The unit of currency is the euro (€), divided into 100 cents. Banknotes are available in denominations of 500, 200, 100, 50, 20, 10 and 5 euros (many shops will not accept €500 notes). There are coins for 2 and 1 euros and for 50, 20, 10, 5, 2 and 1 cent.

ATMs. ATMs are the easiest, and usually the cheapest, way of obtaining cash in euros, drawn on either your debit or credit card. They are widespread in towns, less so in rural areas.

Banks and currency-exchange offices *(banques; bureaux de change)*. Not all banks have exchange facilities; look for those with a change sign. Most banks open Monday to Friday from 9am to 12 noon and 2 to 5pm; some open on Saturday morning and close on Monday. In Monte Carlo, a *bureau de change* opposite the casino is open every day. Big hotels will usually change currency, but the rate is less favourable. The exchange rate often depends on the amount of currency purchased.

Credit cards *(cartes de crédit)*. Most hotels, restaurants, shops, car-hire firms and tourist-related businesses accept the major credit cards, as do motorway toll booths *(péages)* and petrol stations. Several UK credit card companies including Halifax, Nationwide and the Post Office don't charge commission on purchases made abroad and, when paying this way, the exchange rate is usually very favourable.

Official prices are always posted prominently in public establishments, including cafés, bars, hotels and restaurants.

> Could you give me some (small) change? **Pouvez-vous me donner de la (petite) monnaie?**
> I want to change some pounds/dollars. **Je voudrais changer des livres sterling/des dollars.**
> Can I pay with this credit card? **Puis-je payer avec cette carte de crédit?**

O

OPENING TIMES *(heures d'ouverture)*

Opening hours vary greatly, but the main feature is the long Mediterranean lunch break, when most shops close on the dot at noon and do not open again much before 4pm.

Banks are usually open Mon–Fri 9am–noon and 2–5pm. Some may close on Monday or open on Saturday morning. Banking facilities are available at Nice and Marseille airports from early morning to late at night (depending on flight arrivals and departures).

Main post offices are open Mon–Fri 9am–noon and 2–5pm, Sat 9am–noon. In large towns they may open earlier and close later.

Groceries, bakeries and **food shops** are open approximately Mon–Sat 8am–noon and 2, 3 or 4–7 or 8pm. Many open on Sunday morning and close one day during the week, often on Monday.

Museums and art galleries are usually open from 10am–noon and 2–6pm (sometimes later in summer). They often close on Monday or Tuesday. Check before visiting.

P

POLICE *(la police)*

In cities and larger towns you will see the blue-uniformed *police munici-pale*, the local police force which keeps order, investigates crime and directs traffic. Outside the main towns are the *gendarmes*, who wear blue trousers and black jackets with white belts and are also responsible for traffic and crime investigation. The **CRS** police is a national security force called in for emergencies and special occasions.

Call **17** anywhere in France for police assistance.

Where's the nearest police station? **Où est le poste de police le plus proche?**

POST OFFICES

Post offices display a sign with a stylised bluebird and the words *La Poste*. In addition to normal mail service, you can make local or long-distance telephone calls, buy *télécartes* (phone cards), and receive or send money at any post office. You can also buy stamps *(timbres)* and *télécartes* at tobacconists (*tabacs*, displaying a red cone outside).

Poste restante (general delivery). If you don't know ahead of time where you'll be staying, you can have your mail addressed to you in any town c/o *Poste restante, Poste centrale*. You can collect it for a small fee on presentation of your passport. Mail is kept for 15 days.

---

express (special delivery) **par exprès**
airmail **par avion**
registered **en recommandé**
Have you any mail for...? **Avez-vous du courrier pour...?**

PUBLIC HOLIDAYS *(jours fériés)*

1 January **Jour de l'An** New Year's Day
1 May **Fête du Travail** Labour Day
8 May **Fête de la Libération** Victory Day (1945)
14 July **Fête Nationale** Bastille Day
15 August **Assomption** Assumption
1 November **Toussaint** All Saints' Day
11 November **Anniversaire de l'Armistice** Armistice Day
25 December **Noël** Christmas
Movable dates:
Lundi de Pâques Easter Monday
Ascension Ascension
Lundi de Pentecôte Whit Monday

R

RELIGION

France is a predominantly Roman Catholic country. Ask your hotel recep-
tionist or the local tourist office for information about the location and times
of services in English. There are English-speaking Protestant churches and
synagogues in Cannes, Menton, Monaco, Nice and St-Raphaël. Non-Catho-
lic services are called *cultes* and Protestant churches are known as *temples.*

Where is the Protestant church/synagogue? **Où se trouve
le temple protestant/la synagogue?**

T

TELEPHONES

Many public telephones only accept *télécartes* (phone cards), which can
be bought at post offices and tobacconists. Be sure to specify if you want

a *carte à puce* (works only in phone boxes) or a *carte à code* (works from any phone). The *cartes à code* tend to have better international rates. Coin phones are rare. You can make local or long-distance calls from a public phone and from cabins inside most post offices.

France uses a 10-digit telephone-number system. All calls within France require the caller to dial all 10 digits of the number, whether it is a local or long-distance call. Most numbers in Paris begin with 01. Numbers on the French Riviera begin with 04. Mobile phone numbers start with 06, while special-rate numbers varying from freephone 0800 to premium rate 0892 start with 08.

When dialling France from outside the country, the initial 0 is omitted. The country code for France is 33. The country code for Monaco is 377. (Monaco is not on the 10-digit system.)

When making overseas calls from within France, dial **00**, followed by the country code and then the number.

Directory enquiries are available from various providers, all starting with 118, including 118000, 118007, 118008 and 118218. A surcharge will usually be added for calls made from your hotel room.

Mobile phones. If you are using a British-based mobile in France, dial as if you are a local subscriber. To call from one British phone to another, use the international code even if you are both in France; it's cheaper to receive calls when abroad than to make them. If you plan to make a lot of calls within France, it's best to buy a SIM card from a French network provider in a local mobile phone shop.

TIME ZONES

France follows Greenwich Mean Time + 1, and between March and October the clocks are put forward one hour. If your country does the same, the time difference remains constant for most of the year.

TIPPING

A 10–15 percent service charge is included in hotel and restaurant bills. (To be sure, check for *service compris* on the bill.) It is also usual to hand hotel porters, filling station attendants, etc, a coin or two for services. The list below gives suggestions as to what to leave.

Hotel porter, per bag: €2
Hotel maid, per week: €5–10
Lavatory attendant: €0.50–1
Taxi driver: 10 percent (optional)
Tour guide, half-day: 10 percent of the tour price

TOILETS

There are free toilets in museums and department stores. If using a toilet in a café, it is polite to order at least a coffee at the bar. Motorway rest areas always have toilets, but they may be of the squat variety.

> Where is the toilet? **Où sont les toilettes?**

TOURIST INFORMATION

French national tourist offices can help you plan your holiday and will supply you with a wide range of maps and brochures. The Maison de France has websites in English on www.franceguide.com.

Australia: Suite 602, 25 90 Pitt Street, Sydney, NSW 2000, tel: 02 9247 4233
Canada: 1080 Avenue McGill College, Suite 1010, Montréal, Quebec H3A 2W9, tel: 514 288 2026; www.ca.france.fr
UK: Lincoln House, 300 High Holborn, London WC1V 7JH, tel: 020 7061 6631; www.uk.france.fr. Irish citizens should also contact this office
US: 444 Madison Avenue, New York, NY10022, tel: 212 838 7800

Local tourist information offices *(offices du tourisme)* are invaluable sources of information in all French towns. They are usually found near the town centre. Opening hours vary, but the general rule is 8.30 or 9am to noon and from 2 to 6 or 7pm every day except Sunday. Smaller villages may only have a *syndicat d'initiative* with more limited opening hours. Here are a few main addresses:

Antibes–Juan-les-Pins: 42 Avenue Robert Soleau, 06600 Antibes, tel: 04 22 10 60 10, www.antibesjuanlespins.com

Cannes: Palais des Festivals, La Croisette, 06400 Cannes, tel: 04 92 99 84 22, www.cannes-destination.com/tourist-office

Monaco: 2a boulevard des Moulins, Monte Carlo, MC 98030, tel: 377-92 16 61 16, www.visitmonaco.com

Nice: 5 promenade des Anglais, 06000 Nice, tel: 08 92 70 74 07, www.nicetourisme.com

Toulon: 12 place Louis Blanc 83000 Toulon, tel: 04 94 18 53 00, www.toulontourisme.com

TRANSPORT

Buses/coaches *(autobus, autocars)*. There are excellent urban and in-ter-town services all along the French Riviera. Pay as you enter or buy a book of tickets from the driver, and be sure to validate your ticket on board the bus. For details of buses in and around Nice, contact Ligne d'Azur (3 place Masséna, Nice, tel: 08 10 06 10 06, www.lignedazur. com), and for services in the Var contact Sodetrav (tel: 08 25 00 06 50); otherwise contact local tourist offices and bus stations *(gares routières)*.

Taxis are widely available, and all have meters. Taxis in Nice can be very expensive.

Trains. The TER regional network links the coastal towns, with branch lines inland from Cannes to Grasse and Nice to Cuneo in Italy; see www. ter-sncf.com/paca. Enquire about various categories of tickets for tour-ists, children, families, under-26s and OAPs. Eurail passes and Inter-rail cards are valid. See also www.en.oui.sncf.fr.

Trams. A tramway opened in Nice in 2007 and is currently being expanded.

Boat ferries operate from *gares maritimes* (ferry stations) at Cannes for the Iles de Lérins, and for the Iles d'Hyères from Toulon, Hyères/ Giens, Le Lavandou and Cavalaire. In addition, you can take a *bateau-taxi* from Hyères (tel: 04 94 58 31 19). Boats also operate between Ste-Maxime and St-Tropez (tel: 04 94 49 29 39, www.bateauxverts.com)

and St-Raphaël and St-Tropez (tel: 04 94 95 17 46, www.bateauxsaint raphael.com).

The French Riviera pass (a pass which allows free access to a number of sights and activities) is available with an additional transportation option (for an additional €4) to allow unlimited travel on the Nice Cote d'Azur Metropole travel network for 24, 48 or 72 hours. Passes can be bought at a number of outlets including the Nice Tourist Office and a number of hotels.

V

VISAS AND ENTRY REQUIREMENTS

British visitors need only a passport to enter France, as do nationals of other EU countries and Switzerland. Non-EU citizens should check with the French Embassy in their country for entry requirements.

As France is part of the EU, free exchange of non-duty-free goods for personal use is permitted between France, the UK and the Republic of Ireland. However, duty-free items are still subject to restrictions – see http://france.visahq.co.uk/customs.

For residents of non-EU countries, find out what you can and cannot bring back into your country at www.iatatravelcentre.com (under Customs, Currency & Airport information).

W

WEBSITES AND INTERNET ACCESS

Wi-Fi is available at numerous hotels and bars and at Nice airport.

The following list is a selection of websites, providing useful information about the French Riviera and further inland in Provence.

www.beyond.fr

www.cote.azur.fr

www.uk.france.fr

www.en.nicetourisme.com

RECOMMENDED HOTELS

The French Riviera has a large number of establishments catering to all tastes. In high season, however, accommodation can be booked up, and you are advised to reserve well in advance.

Our selection is based on geographical location and quality of accommodation. (Some of the restaurants listed also have rooms, see page 106) To give you an indication of price, we have used the symbols below for the average cost of a double room per night, in high season, excluding breakfast (all rooms are with private bath or shower and are air-conditioned unless stated). Prices may be lower out of season, but may well go up for special events, such as the Monaco Grand Prix and the Cannes Film Festival. Many hotels also have triple or family rooms, or can add a bed (sometimes for a fee) for a child. The traditional breakfast of coffee, baguette and croissants is increasingly being replaced by a generous buffet; expect the price to be proportional to that of the hotel, from around €6 in a budget hotel to €20 or more in a luxury one.

All the hotels listed take major credit cards unless stated otherwise.

€€€€	€260–380
€€€	€160–260
€€	€80–160
€	under €80

ANTIBES

Mas Djoliba €€ *29 avenue de Provence, 06600 Antibes, tel: 04 93 34 02 48*, www.hotel-djoliba.com. Pretty Provençal-style hotel, within walking distance of the old town and beach. It has 13 bedrooms, a garden and a pool. Closed mid-Nov–Feb.

BORMES-LES-MIMOSAS

Hôtel Bellevue €€ *14 place Gambetta, 83230 Bormes-les-Mimosas, tel: 04 94 71 15 15*, www.bellevuebormes.com. An amber-coloured, 15-room hotel-restaurant set on the main square of the old village with views down to the coast and a busy restaurant downstairs. Closed mid-Nov–mid-Jan. Accepts MasterCard and Visa only.

CANNES

Carlton Intercontinental €€€€ *58 La Croisette, 06400 Cannes, tel: 04 93 06 40 06,* www.ihg.com. Prestigious hotel with 343 luxurious bedrooms and 39 suites. Elegant *belle époque* architecture, private beach, health club, swimming pool, conference facilities and parking. Houses two restaurants: Carlton Restaurant and Carlton Beach Restaurant.

Hôtel Chanteclair € *12 rue Forville, 06400 Cannes, tel: 04 93 39 68 88,* www.hotelchanteclair.fr. This budget hotel with 15 simply furnished rooms near the famous market is one of the few hotels in the old town. Breakfast is served in the flower-filled courtyard in summer.

Hôtel Splendid €€€ *4–6 rue Félix Faure, 06400 Cannes, tel: 04 97 06 22 22,* www.splendid-hotel-cannes.com. A sparkling white *belle époque* edifice in the heart of the action, near the port and almost opposite the Palais des Festivals. The 62 rooms have been comfortably updated while retaining period flourishes; breakfast is served on a large sunny terrace.

Ruc Hôtel €€ *15 boulevard de Strasbourg, 06400 Cannes, tel: 04 92 98 33 60,* www.ruc-hotel.com. Elegant hotel done out in 18th-century style, with 30 well-decorated bedrooms, some of which open onto a courtyard garden. A top-floor terrace has views over the hills. There is a tennis club and swimming pool next door, and secured public parking nearby. No restaurant but breakfast is available to be delivered to your room.

LA CROIX VALMER

La Pinède Plage €€€€ *Plage de Gigaro, 83420 La Croix Valmer, tel: 04 94 55 16 16,* www.pinedeplage.com. Pastel-coloured neo-Provençal rooms, some with balconies overlooking the sea, set amid parasol pines directly on the sandy Plage de Gigaro. Free hire of bicycles, kayaks, pedalos and windsurfs for hotel guests, with the possibility of jet-skiing, water-skiing and boat hire. Guests have the use of the spa at sister establishment Château de Valmer. Closed mid-Oct–mid-Apr.

EZE

La Bastide aux Camélias €€ *23C route de l'Adret, 06360 Eze, tel: 04 93 41 13 68, www.bastideauxcamelias.com.* On the outskirts of Eze in a lovely rural location, this 16th-century farmhouse has been turned into a stylish four-bedroom B&B by its French owners. Enjoy a dip in the pool before heading to the treatment cabin for an aromatherapy massage.

Château Eza €€€€ *rue de la Pise, 06360 Eze, tel: 04 93 41 12 24, www.chateaueza.com.* Perched high over the Mediterranean, this has to be one of the most romantic hotels on the Riviera. In a medieval building built into the ramparts of Eze, the 12 bedrooms have pretty *toile de jouy* print fabrics, many have exposed stone walls and stone fireplaces, and some have terraces. There's a sleek bar, and a gastronomic restaurant with spectacular views. No access to vehicles. Closed Nov–mid-Dec.

FRÉJUS

Hôtel L'Arena €€ *139–145 rue du Général de Gaulle, 83600 Fréjus, tel: 04 94 17 09 40, www.hotel-frejus-arena.com.* With 39 ochre-tinted, Provençal-style rooms housed in three renovated villas, this is the nicest hotel in Fréjus old town. The inviting pool is shaded by 100-year-old palm trees while the gourmet restaurant is popular with guests and locals. Extra charge for use of car park.

GRIMAUD

La Boulangerie €€ *route de Collobrières, 83310 Grimaud, tel: 04 94 43 23 16, www.hotel-laboulangerie.com.* Quiet site 5km (3 miles) from the coast. This Provençal hotel has 11 lovely bedrooms and gardens with a pool and tennis court. Fine views over the Maures mountains. Closed mid-Oct–Easter.

HYÈRES

Hôtel BOR €€ *3 allée Emile Gérard, Les Pesquiers, 83400 Hyères, tel: 04 94 58 02 73,* www.hotel-bor.com. The name stands for Beau Original Rare, and this friendly, small hotel has been stylishly refurbished with waxed concrete, decking and subtle lighting. Situated on the beach, you can walk straight into the sea from the waterside terrace. Lunch in the restaurant and head to the cocktail bar at night. Closed Nov–Feb.

ILES D'HYÈRES

L'Auberge des Glycines €€€ *22 place d'Armes, Ile de Porquerolles, 83400 Hyères, tel: 04 94 58 30 36,* www.auberge-glycines.com. Access to the island is by ferry or *bateau-taxi* from the Presqu'ile de Giens, Cavalaire or Toulon (cars are not allowed on the island). This 11-bedroom Provençal inn is set in pretty gardens overlooking the village square. The restaurant specialises in local cuisine, especially fish.

JUAN-LES-PINS

Belles Rives €€€€ *33 boulevard Baudoin, 06160 Juan-les-Pins, tel: 04 93 61 02 79,* www.bellesrives.com. On the beach with views over the Cap d'Antibes, the 42-room villa retains all the charm of the 1930s, when it was the home of F. Scott Fitzgerald. It has a private sandy beach and two restaurants (**€€€**): the gastronomic La Passagère and a summer beach restaurant. Closed Jan–Mar.

Les Mimosas €€ *rue Pauline, 06160 Juan-les-Pins, tel: 04 93 61 04 16,* www.hotelmimosas.com. A large early 20th-century house set in quiet palm-tree-filled gardens just a 5-minute walk from the beach. It has thirty-four attractive bedrooms, plus a swimming pool and private parking. No restaurant. Closed Oct–Apr.

MENTON

Hôtel Lemon € *10 rue Albert 1er, 06500 Menton, tel: 04 93 28 63 63,* www. hotel-lemon.com. Eco-friendly hotel housed in a tall 19th-century villa with 18 refurbished rooms in contemporary style. Breakfast is mainly organic and served in a garden shaded by palms and citrus trees.

MONACO

Ambassador Hotel €€ *10 Avenue Prince Pierre de Monaco, 98000 Monaco, tel. 04 97 97 96 96,* www.ambassadormonaco.com. Located at the base of the Rock of Monaco, this well positioned hotel is close to the Prince's Palace, the Monte Carlo Casino, and just a few steps from the bustling market place on Place d'Armes. The hotel offers comfortable rooms and friendly service through the year.

MOUGINS

Hôtel Lune de Mougins €€ *1082 avenue du Général de Gaulle, 06250 Mougins, tel: 04 93 75 77 33,* www.hotel-lunedemougins.com. Elegant hotel and spa whose 45 rooms and public areas are decorated in contemporary Provençal style. The garden, filled with olive, cypress and pine trees, has a pool and terrace. The restaurant serves Provençal cuisine each evening while the lounge bar is open all day.

NICE

Hôtel Aria €€ *15 avenue Auber, 06000 Nice, tel: 04 93 88 30 69,* www.aria-nice.fr. This good-value, renovated 19th-century hotel overlooks an attractive garden square amid the *belle époque* and Art Deco buildings of the new town. The thirty rooms are light, have high ceilings and are decorated in sunny colours. No restaurant.

Hôtel Rex € *3 rue Masséna, 06000 Nice, tel: 04 93 87 87 38,* www.hotel-rex.com. A small, tastefully decorated budget hotel in the centre of town yet in a quiet location. Once off the busy main street, the pastel-coloured rooms are reached by a bridge over a courtyard. All rooms have free Wi-Fi.

Hôtel Suisse €€€ *15 quai Raubà Capéù, 06300 Nice, tel: 04 92 17 39 00,* www.hotel-nice-suisse.com. At the far eastern end of the promenade des Anglais, this 38-room hotel offers wonderful views from its 35 sea-front rooms; some have balconies, all have Wi-Fi. Décor is bright and contemporary. No restaurant or car park.

Negresco €€€€ *37 promenade des Anglais, 06000 Nice, tel: 04 93 16 64 00*, www.hotel-negresco-nice.com. One of the world's great hotels, built in 1912 and marvellously situated on the promenade, with a private beach just across the street. Flamboyant *belle époque* architecture and 114 magnificent bedrooms and apartments furnished with antiques. The celebrated Chantecler restaurant is acknowledged as one of the best (and most expensive) tables in the region (closed Jan). La Rotonde is a less formal brasserie, serving until midnight. Valet parking.

Windsor €€–€€€ *11 rue Dalpozzo, 06000 Nice, tel: 04 93 88 59 35*, www.hotelwindsornice.com. Wonderfully characterful hotel, close to the centre and seafront. Fifty-seven comfortable bedrooms, most of which are air-conditioned, some with balconies; the best have been individually decorated by internationally renowned contemporary artists, including Varini, Ben and Lily van der Stokker. Dinner is served in the lovely bar or in the garden in summer. Has a small but gorgeous tropical garden with swimming pool, as well as a Turkish spa, gymnasium and parking.

PLAN-DE-LA-TOUR

Mas des Brugassières €€ *83120 Plan-de-la-Tour, tel: 04 94 55 50 55*, www.mas-des-brugassieres.com. Built in the 1970s in an attractive, rustic Provençal style in the Maures hills, 1.5km (1 mile) outside the village. The 11 bedrooms are fresh and cool, with traditional tiled floors, some opening onto the garden and swimming pool. No restaurant. Closed mid-Oct–end April.

RAMATUELLE

La Ferme d'Augustin €€€€ *plage de Tahiti, 83350 Ramatuelle, tel: 04 94 55 97 00*, www.fermeaugustin.com. Set in vineyards next to Tahiti Beach, this friendly family-run hotel in a lovely old farmhouse is surrounded by luxuriant gardens. The 46 bedrooms overlook the gardens and many have balconies and sea views. The restaurant, for guests only, uses produce from the hotel's own kitchen garden. There is a heated swimming pool and secured parking. Most guests are regulars so reserve well ahead. Closed mid-Oct–Mar.

Kon Tiki Village €€ *route des Plages, 083350 Ramatuelle, tel: 04 94 55 96 96*, www.riviera-villages.com. Family-oriented resort at the water's edge with thatched cabins sleeping 4–6 people. As well as a choice of five restaurants, there is also a spa, a market and a variety of activities on offer. The company also has two other villages (Prairies de la Mer and Toison d'Or) nearby. Closed Nov–Mar.

ST-JEAN-CAP-FERRAT

Brise Marine €€€ *58 avenue Jean Mermoz, 06230 St-Jean-Cap-Ferrat, tel: 04 93 76 04 36*, www.hotel-brisemarine.com. Eighteen fairly small but immaculate bedrooms reside in this authentic, late 19th-century villa situated overlooking the Mediterranean. A steeply terraced garden adorned with palm trees, fountains and flowerpots leads down to the sea. No restaurant. Closed Nov–Mar.

Hôtel Patricia €€ *avenue de l'Ange Gardien, 06230 Villefranche-sur-Mer, tel: 04 93 01 06 70*, www.hotel-patricia.riviera.fr. Delightful 10-room budget hotel in a terracotta-coloured villa on the Villefranche side of Cap Ferrat. Soak up the rays in the Mediterranean garden then take a dip in the Jacuzzi. It's a short stroll to the public and private beaches.

ST-PAUL-DE-VENCE

Hôtel Le Hameau €€€ *528 route de La Colle, 06570 St-Paul-de-Vence, tel: 04 93 32 80 24*, www.le-hameau.com. An 18th-century whitewashed farmhouse set in terraced orange and lemon groves just outside the town. Seventeen comfortable bedrooms and apartments attractively decorated in rustic Provençal style, some with a terrace. There is a swimming pool, a small fitness room and parking. No restaurant. Closed mid-Nov–mid-Feb.

ST-RAPHAËL

Chancellor Golf-Hôtel Valescure €€ *55 avenue Paul l'Hermite, 83700 St-Raphaël, tel: 09 70 38 29 62, www.valescure.najeti.fr.* Located on a sports and golf complex 5km (3 miles) outside town, this modern hotel has light, airy bedrooms, a new wing with spacious suites, and a restaurant. Gardens include a pool and tennis courts. Special golf packages available.

ST-TROPEZ

Hôtel Lou Cagnard €€ *18 avenue Paul Roussel, 83990 St-Tropez, tel: 04 94 97 04 24, www.hotel-lou-cagnard.com.* A friendly, simple family-run hotel in an old village house in a leafy garden close to the town centre. Some of the 18 rooms are air-conditioned; the cheapest rooms don't have en-suite toilets. Has private parking. Only accepts MasterCard and Visa. Closed Nov–Dec.

Le Yaca €€€€ *1 boulevard d'Aumale, 83990 St-Tropez, tel: 04 94 55 81 00, www.hotel-le-yaca.fr.* Twenty-five comfortable bedrooms in an elegant 200-year-old house situated in the old town, between the port and the Citadelle. Some rooms have a terrace overlooking the sea, or the garden with its swimming pool. There is a restaurant onsite and valet parking nearby. Closed Nov–Easter. Its owners also run the more contemporary Le Y (avenue Paul Signac, tel: 04 94 55 55 15).

STE-MAXIME

Citotel Hostellerie de la Nartelle € *48 avenue Général Touzet du Vigier, 83120 Sainte-Maxime, tel: 04 94 96 73 10.* Right in the centre of town and a one-minute walk to the beach, this hotel offers air-conditioned rooms (some have private balconies), a communal outdoor terrace which overlooks the heated swimming pool and a restaurant.

TOULON

Grand Hôtel Dauphiné € *10 rue Berthelot, 83000 Toulon, tel: 04 94 92 20 28,* www.grandhoteldauphine.com. Well-placed on a pedestrianised street in the old town, the Dauphiné has been pleasantly decorated with brightly coloured fabrics and abstract art work dotted around the otherwise clean and crisp, white canvas.

LE TRAYAS

Le Relais des Calanques €€ *route des Escalles, 83530 Le Trayas, tel: 04 94 44 14 06,* www.relaisdescalanques.fr. Charming, shabby-chic 12-room hotel in a remote location on the Corniche d'Or with direct access to the sea on one side and the Estérel mountains on the other. The restaurant is well known for its seafood, especially *marmite du pêcheur* (fish stew). Closed Oct–Mar.

VENCE

Auberge des Seigneurs €€ *place du Frêne, 06140 Vence, tel: 04 93 58 04 24,* www.auberge-seigneurs.com. Adjoining the château in the oldest part of the old town is this small, family-run historic coaching inn. The six Provençal-style bedrooms are named after painters who stayed in Vence. Not air-conditioned but rooms do have fans. The popular restaurant (€€) specialises in local cuisine but is closed Sun–Mon. Ring for details of winter closure.

Hôtel Diana €€ *79 avenue des Poilus, 06140 Vence, tel: 04 93 58 28 56,* www.hotel-diana.fr. This modern hotel on the edge of the old town was tastefully redecorated after a change of ownership back in 2007. More than half of the rooms have a kitchenette. There is a large roof terrace with deckchairs, Jacuzzi and exercise machines. Offers private parking but no restaurant.

VILLEFRANCHE-SUR-MER

Hôtel Welcome €€€ *3 quai Amiral Courbet, 06230 Villefranche-sur-Mer, tel: 04 93 76 27 62,* www.welcomehotel.com. An historic hotel situated on the colourful quayside next to the Cocteau chapel. The thirty-six spacious rooms, all with balconies, overlook the port. There is also a wine bar. Closed mid-Nov–Christmas.

INDEX

INSIGHT ⊙ GUIDES POCKET GUIDE

FRENCH RIVIERA

First Edition 2018

Editor: Sian Marsh
Author: Suzanne Patterson and Meg Jump
Head of DTP and Pre-Press: Rebeka Davies
Picture Editor: Tom Smyth
Cartography Update: Carte
Update Production: Apa Digital
Photography Credits: Alamy 5T; Bigstock
60; Dreamstime 14, 41; Fotolia 42, 67, 76;
iStock 1, 4MC, 4TC, 5TC, 5M, 37, 75; Public
domain 19, 20; Shutterstock 4ML, 5MC;
SuperStock 4TL, 5M, 52; Sylvaine Poitau/Apa
Publications 6L, 6R, 7, 7R, 13, 17, 24, 26, 27,
28, 31, 32, 35, 38, 40, 43, 45, 46, 47, 49, 54, 57,
59, 63, 65, 73, 82, 84, 87, 89, 92, 97, 101, 103;
Villa Noailles/Olivier Amsellem 5MC; Wadey
James/Apa Publications 11, 51, 68, 70, 78,
79, 81, 90, 98
Cover Picture: Shutterstock

Distribution
UK, Ireland and Europe: Apa Publications
(UK) Ltd; sales@insightguides.com
United States and Canada: Ingram
Publisher Services; ips@ingramcontent.com
Australia and New Zealand: Woodslane;
info@woodslane.com.au
Southeast Asia: Apa Publications (SN) Pte;
singaporeoffice@insightguides.com
Worldwide: Apa Publications (UK) Ltd;
sales@insightguides.com

**Special Sales, Content Licensing
and CoPublishing**
Insight Guides can be purchased in bulk
quantities at discounted prices. We can
create special editions, personalised jackets
and corporate imprints tailored to your
needs. sales@insightguides.com;
www.insightguides.biz

Contact us
Every effort has been made to provide
accurate information in this publication,
but changes are inevitable. The publisher
cannot be responsible for any resulting loss,
inconvenience or injury. We would appreciate
it if readers would call our attention to any
errors or outdated information. We also
welcome your suggestions; please contact
us at: hello@insightguides.com
www.insightguides.com